Keith Norfleet

BEYOND THE SHADOWS

© Keith Norfleet 2025

All rights reserved. No part of this book may be reproduced, stored in a retrieval system, or transmitted in any form or by any means, electronic, mechanical, photocopying, recording, or otherwise, without the prior written permission of the author.

Keith Norfleet
Mt. Juliet, Tennessee
keithnorfleet85@gmail.com

This book is a memoir based on the author's personal recollections of real events. While great care has been taken to provide an accurate account, some names, locations, and details have been changed, fictionalized, or reconstructed to protect the privacy of individuals. Certain conversations and events are based on the author's best recollection and may not reflect exact words or actions. This book represents the author's subjective experiences and interpretations, and is not intended to serve as an authoritative or investigative account of any events or individuals.

The author and publisher make no claims to the absolute accuracy of events depicted and accept no liability for any perceived misrepresentations. Any resemblance to real persons, living or deceased, outside of public figures, is purely coincidental. This work is not intended to harm, defame, or misrepresent any individual, and any such interpretations are unintentional.

This book is dedicated to anyone who was affected by the tragic event that occurred on July 4th, 2009. To anyone who knew Jenny or Steve and to the loved ones who lost them and felt you were left with more questions than answers.

This book is for you.

PROLOGUE

If you're reading this, I want to start by saying thank you.

This isn't just a book. This is my life. My pain. My love. My loss. My truth.

For years, I kept so much of this buried deep inside of me. I let the world tell it version of my story while I stayed silent, convincing myself that silence was safer, that it was better to just move on. But the truth has a way of weighing on you. The things left unsaid don't just disappear—they linger. They grow heavier with time.

I never set out to write a book. Honestly, I never thought I could. But after everything—the documentaries, the media stories, the misunderstandings, the outright lies—I realized that no one else was ever going to tell this story the way it deserved to be told. No one else was going to tell Jenny's story the way it deserved to be told.

So I decided to do it myself.

This book isn't just about what happened in 2009. It's about who Jenny was, who I was, and how we found each other and fell in love long before that tragedy changed everything.

It's about the unanswered questions that still haunt me, the things I saw and experienced that no one ever asked me about, and the pieces of this story that were conveniently ignored by those who wanted to wrap it all up in a neat, simple narrative.

But this book is also about what came after. It's about grief, guilt, and the years I spent trying to outrun a pain that I never truly faced. It's about the mistakes I made, the lessons I learned, and the long road I walked to get to where I am now.

If you've ever loved someone and lost them, if you've ever felt misunderstood, if you've ever struggled to make peace with your past—then maybe this book is for you, too.

I don't have all the answers. I probably never will. But what I do have is my truth. And after all these years, I'm finally ready to share it.

So here it is.

This is my story. This is her story.

This is our story.

And this time, I'm telling it my way.

CHAPTER 1

ANTIOCH, TENNESSEE

Antioch was a place with two sides. To some, it was just another suburb of Nashville, but to those who grew up there, it was a world of its own--a dangerous, unpredictable place where choices could define the rest of your life.

For me, Antioch was both a playground and a battleground. It's where I first discovered the thrill of competition, the sting of disappointment, and the dangerous allure of easy money. What I didn't realize at the time was how deeply Antioch would shape the decisions and events that would follow me for years to come.

Growing up in the shadows of the rundown apartment complex, Apollo Apartments in lower Antioch, I found my comfort in playing and watching sports with my friends. Almost every day, I'd gather outside with my closest friends to play any sport from sunup to sundown, and if the streetlights worked or the moon was bright enough, we'd keep playing well into the night. The games were intense, fueled by our fiery tempers and competitive nature. Arguments were as common as buckets, and on more than one occasion, we walked away from the court angrier than when we arrived, but we always came back. Those games weren't just a way to pass the time--they were an escape, a way to channel the frustrations of growing up in a place that didn't offer much hope.

Despite its challenges, plenty of people found a way to make it out and build something for themselves. Artists such as Jelly Roll and Yelawolf would later turn their struggles into stories, using music that resonated with millions, capturing the grind of growing up here. While I wasn't friends with either of them early on, we shared mutual friends growing up and often ended up at the same parties or clubs on weekends before they became famous. Brandon Miller would later make his way out through basketball and all the way to the NBA and Casey Atwood would find his path in NASCAR. Their success is comforting to know--it proves that those childhood dreams weren't just dreams. They can become a reality for kids growing up there with similar struggles as long as they keep dreaming and never give up. Unfortunately for me though, I traded those dreams in for quick money, and my life veered in a completely different direction because of it.

At home, life wasn't very easy. My dad was around, but not in the way I needed him to be. His strained relationship with my mom kept him at a distance, leaving my sisters to pick up the slack. Josette, who I call Bootsie, the oldest, had a fierce, protective streak, while Crystal, known to me as Leeanne, was always supportive in her own way. Both of them kept me grounded during times when I could've easily lost my way.

Like every kid in Antioch, I had big dreams--college, sports, maybe even something more. I dabbled in school sports, inspired by the games I played with my friends. But as I got older, the pull of quick and easy money became stronger. What started as smoking weed with friends spiraled into something much darker. By the time I was a teenager, I was popping all sorts of pills, selling any drugs available, and hanging with all the wrong people. At first, it felt empowering--money in my pocket and respect around my neighborhood. But that illusion didn't last long.

The robberies were my wake-up call. The first one happened shortly after I got off the school bus coming home from Antioch High School. I'd made it a habit to sell anything I had under the radar at school between classes and apparently word got around to the wrong people and a grown man was waiting for me at the bus stop because of it. The fear that gripped me that day with his gun to my head was unlike anything I'd ever felt before. Luckily he ran off with just my backpack and what I had left that day that I hadn't sold and nothing more ever came from it. The second robbery, though, was on the porch of my mom's apartment. A gun in my face over a few dollars or a bag of weed made me realize how close to home this had become and just how quickly everything could end. This game didn't care who you were or what you thought you had. It would take it all--and it almost took me.

Leeanne saw what was happening before I did. She didn't sugarcoat it. "If you don't get out of here Keith, you're going to end up dead." She was right, and I knew it. After that second robbery, her words were impossible to ignore. She and her husband offered me a way out: a chance to leave Antioch and start over in Florida. Looking back now, I wonder where I'd be if I hadn't listened to her. It's not something I like to think about often.

Leaving wasn't easy. My brother-in-law arrived to pick me up, and I can still see my mom standing there as we loaded the truck. She was upset, sad, and angry all at once. Her arms were crossed, tears in her eyes, but she didn't try to stop me. I was the last to leave home and once I was gone she would be all alone but we both knew I had to go. If I stayed, there wouldn't be much of me left to save.

As the truck pulled away, I looked back one last time at the neighborhood that had both raised and nearly destroyed me. Antioch helped shape me into the man I would become, but it also took pieces of me I'd never get back. I didn't know what Florida would hold, but I knew one thing: it was my chance to start over, and I wasn't going to waste it.

CHAPTER 2

A NEW BEGINNING IN FLORIDA

As nervous as I was about leaving everything I had known behind—my friends and family—I couldn't deny the excitement building within me. While I had grown comfortable with my life in Antioch, running the streets, playing basketball, and chasing girls, there was always a part of me that envied the kids who lived near the beach. Their simple, carefree lives felt like the opposite of everything I'd known, and moving to Florida seemed like my chance to embrace that lifestyle for myself.

I couldn't wait to trade in my baggy clothes for surf shorts and flip-flops and swap my basketball for a surfboard. Growing up, I'd grown up watching cartoons like Rocket Power and movies like Johnny Tsunami, dreaming of a life surrounded by sand and waves. For the first time in years, it felt like I was stepping toward something new and full of possibility.

When I arrived, that excitement mixed with a sense of urgency. My brother-in-law and sister understood that adjusting to this new life would take time, but I was determined to show them I could pull my weight. Those first few weeks weren't about making friends or pursuing an education—they were about finding a job, helping out financially, and saving for a car. I knew that once I laid that foundation, I could start focusing on everything else Florida had to offer.

Living with my sister and brother-in-law was exactly what I needed during those early days in Florida. It felt liberating to be in a space where I could start becoming the young man I wanted to be. They treated me like an equal most of the time, but when needed, they stepped in as the big sister and big brother I could always count on.

My brother-in-law quickly became both a good friend and the big brother figure I'd never had before. He was there to guide me, but also to joke around and make me feel at ease in this new environment. Leeanne, on the other hand, remained the protective big sister she had always been. She looked out for my best interests and didn't shy away from being critical or honest when she thought I needed it.

Her advice was always thoughtful, and while I didn't always want to hear it, I knew she was coming from a place of love.

We shared a lot of good times together. They were both in the military and doing well financially, which meant we had the opportunity to travel and explore places I'd never imagined visiting. Whether it was road trips or trying new experiences, they made sure I felt included and exposed to a world far beyond what I'd known in Antioch. For the first time, I was beginning to see what life could look like if I kept moving forward.

The first friend I met in Florida was Quan. We were around the same age and at similar stages in life, both trying to figure out our next steps. Quan was living with his dad and preparing to join the military, while I was focused on finding a job and contributing to my new household. After we met, we started hanging out regularly, walking around town and looking for work.

It wasn't long before Quan introduced me to a group of friends that would come to mean a lot to me. There was Daren, who shared my love for basketball, and his younger brother Jon Jon, who I connected with on a deeper level.

They were transplants from Kansas, but their personalities couldn't have been more different. Then there was John—better known as "White John" because there were so many Johns—who quickly became one of my closest friends and someone I still proudly call a friend to this day. John, originally from Arizona, had military roots and was living with his grandparents at the time. Like Quan, he was also new to Florida.

What bonded us was our shared experience of being outsiders, trying to make sense of this new place. The only difference was that they were all still in high school, while I had recently dropped out. That dynamic meant our time together revolved around their school schedules, but it also made me realize how much I missed being in school.

We were inseparable for much of my time in Florida. Whether we were at the mall chasing girls, watching every movie that hit the theaters, or playing basketball endlessly, we did everything together. They weren't just my friends—they were my support system. And, ultimately, it was their influence that pushed me to go back to school and earn my high school diploma at Orange Park High.

My sister and brother-in-law couldn't have been more supportive when I decided to go back to school. They knew how much I had struggled with the decision to drop out in Antioch and how deeply it had affected me. They were happy to see me taking steps to reclaim a part of myself I thought I'd lost.

Both of them pitched in to help make it happen. Whether it was driving me themselves or letting me borrow their car or truck, they made sure I had everything I needed to succeed. At first, I signed up for a GED program, thinking that would be the quickest way to move forward. But after taking an assessment test, I was advised to enroll in a program to earn my actual high school diploma from Orange Park High School.

Hearing that was a game changer. I was ecstatic—and so was my sister and my brother-in-law. They saw it as a fresh start for me, and their encouragement made all the difference. I threw myself into the program and eventually earned my high school diploma. Ironically, I managed to graduate a full year before my original class in Antioch. I couldn't help but laugh about it and would call my friends back home to brag. It was a small victory, but it felt monumental in my journey to rebuild my life.

Earning my high school diploma felt like a turning point. For the first time, college was back on the table, something I'd thought was no longer an option. But even with that possibility, I felt a strong sense of urgency to get a job and contribute. My sister and brother-in-law had been so supportive, and I didn't want to take that for granted. We talked about college a lot, but we also knew that pursuing it would make it harder to maintain a full-time job.

My sister reassured me that whatever I chose to do, she had my back. Still, I felt stuck between wanting to better myself and needing to help out financially. After weighing my options, I decided to focus on either full-time work or the military. The more I researched the military, the more appealing it seemed. My sister and brother-in-law's lifestyle was a big inspiration—they were financially stable, had freedom, and seemed relatively stress-free. Of course, they were honest about the ups and downs of military life, but their overall experience made it look like a good path.

I decided to enlist, and my sister and brother-in-law did everything they could to help. Unfortunately, I was paired with a recruiter who was close to retirement and seemed disinterested in helping me succeed.

He didn't go out of his way like other recruiters did, and I ended up in a situation where I'd have to go through a two-year unpaid program before I could even attend boot camp. It didn't make sense, and since I couldn't switch recruiters, I reluctantly backed out of the military path.

That left me with one option: a full-time, 9-to-5 job. But even that didn't come easily. The local job market was tough, and the only position I could find was an overnight shift at BJ's Wholesale Club, working in a freezer. It was miserable. Every minute of it felt like a punishment. I stuck it out for a few grueling months, hating every aspect of the job. Then one day, my brother-in-law came into my room while I was still asleep.

"Get up," he said. "We're going to the beach."

I told him I had to work, and he just laughed. "Do you like that job?" he asked.

"No, I hate it," I admitted.

"Okay then," he said. "There are a ton of other jobs out there. Quit, and let's go to the beach."

And that's exactly what I did. I quit my job, and we spent the day at the beach.

After quitting BJ's, I decided to revisit the idea of college and even enrolled at FSCJ. But as much as I wanted to pursue it, reality set in again. A full-time job opportunity came up, and with my need to save for a car, I couldn't justify the time and financial commitment college required. Instead, I took a job working overnight stock at Winn-Dixie. It wasn't glamorous, but I was familiar with the work from my time at Food Lion back in Antioch, and, thankfully, this job didn't involve working in a freezer.

I stayed at Winn-Dixie while I worked on solving my transportation problem. My sister had just upgraded to a new car, and we worked out a deal for me to take her old one. Having a car changed everything. Suddenly, I felt like I was finally making progress. My focus shifted from surviving to taking the next big step—getting my own place.

The idea of moving out made me nervous. It felt like such a monumental step, and I wasn't sure I was ready for it. I talked to my sister about it constantly, and she reassured me that I was ready for this new challenge. Her encouragement gave me the push I needed to start planning for what came next.

During this time, my work schedule at Winn-Dixie meant I was spending less time with friends. Despite that, John and I grew closer, and he quickly became my closest friend in the group. It was John who introduced me to Megan. At the time, I wasn't looking for a relationship, but meeting her changed that almost instantly.

When I first met Megan, she was a year or two younger than me, likely a sophomore in high school while I would have been a senior. Even though I thought she was pretty, I was reluctant to talk to her like that. For one, John kind of had a crush on her at the time, which is why we were hanging out with her in the first place. I didn't want to step on his toes.

Over time, we hung out so much in our free time that Megan and I really hit it off. Our personalities clicked, and eventually, John's crush faded as he started talking to someone else. That gave Megan and me the chance to spend more time together one-on-one. The more we hung out, the more I found myself really liking her and thinking about taking things to the next level.

Unfortunately, before we could get there, family matters forced Megan to move back to West Virginia. Her leaving caught me completely off guard. I hadn't realized how attached I'd become to her until she was gone. It hit me in a way I hadn't experienced before and sent me into a pretty deep depression that really caught me off guard. I opened up to my sister about how I was feeling, and it was the first time I really addressed depression in my life. I'd always thought of it as something everyone dealt with, but losing Megan was the point that exposed just how much I'd been carrying.

Megan and I stayed in touch over the phone for a while and even talked about the possibility of moving in together and getting an apartment. We had these conversations for weeks, but eventually, reality set in for both of us. It just wasn't going to happen. The phone calls became fewer and farther between until they stopped altogether.

Around the same time, it seemed like everyone else in my life was leaving too. Darren and Jon Jon moved back to Kansas, Quan returned to South Carolina, and John joined the Navy. Before I knew it, I was back to square one with friends. I had no other choice but to shift my focus back to work and trying to get my own place.

Not long after, I met Nick, who would go on to become one of my best friends. He lived in the same apartment complex the entire time I had been there, but we'd never hung out before. Nick was an extreme introvert, so we didn't connect until one day when I was outside smoking a cigarette and something sparked a conversation.

We quickly became inseparable, bonding over a shared passion for music. Nick got me back into writing and recording, and I even recorded my first (terrible) song on my sister's computer. Through music, our friendship grew, and Nick eventually introduced me to some of his other friends, including Isaiah. It was Isaiah who would later introduce me to Jenny.

Unfortunately, Nick is no longer with us. After I moved back to Tennessee with Jenny, we lost touch. Years later, while on a trip to Colorado with my friend Joe, I looked him up on Facebook and found out he had passed away.

The time I spent with Nick was unlike any other friendship I'd ever had. Our shared passion for music was the core of everything we did. We'd spend hours debating rap and hip hop, arguing over who was the greatest of all time and the best artists from the South, North, East, and West. Nick and I shared a lot of the same opinions, and our contrasting styles when writing and recording complemented each other perfectly on the tracks we made together. Nick was incredibly talented, with a style that was uniquely his. Even now, I strongly believe that if we, along with Joe, had stuck to it, we would have made it big in music.

Unfortunately, our inconsistent commitment to music became our downfall. We'd go through periods where we took it seriously, followed by times when we completely stopped caring. I still listen to some of the tracks we recorded back then, and every time, I shake my head, wondering what could have been if we had stayed the course.

Nick was more than just a friend and collaborator—he was a part of my life with Jenny, too. After Isaiah introduced me to Jenny, Nick quickly became close to both of us. He never minded third-wheeling on dates or hanging out with us at the beach.

There's one day with Nick and Jenny that I'll never forget, a memory that brings a tear to my eye even now. We were at the beach together, enjoying a day off, when Nick asked us if we ever thought about death and when we thought we were going to die. The question caught me off guard, and I told him to change the subject. Jenny laughed and teased him, saying, "Way to bring the day down, Nick." We all laughed, but Nick's response stayed with me. He said he'd always assumed he would die young.

I told him that was depressing and pushed to move on, but then Jenny chimed in, saying she had always felt the same way. I looked at them both, shook my head, and said, "Well, neither one of y'all are dying. You better stay with me because I'm not losing anybody else." We laughed it off and spent the rest of the day enjoying the beach. Later, I hugged Jenny and told her, "I don't know what I'd do if you died. You better not ever die." She smiled, kissed me, and said, "You don't have anything to worry about."

Considering everything that's happened—losing both Nick and Jenny—that day and that conversation have stayed with me. I think about it often, and I know I'll carry it with me for the rest of my life.

After Nick introduced me to Isaiah, he quickly became a good friend. Nick had moved to Georgia so Isaiah and I started hanging out more often. I had the car, so he would come with me to the mall where we'd shop, catch a movie, or talk to girls. Isaiah wasn't into sports or music like some of my other friends, but he was a steady presence—a good friend who was always there when I didn't want to be alone.

One evening, while we were at the mall, Isaiah got a phone call. It was a friend of his, a girl who needed a ride home after work. When he hung up, he asked me if we could pick her up. I jokingly asked why she was calling him for a ride when he didn't have a car. Laughing, he said, "She thinks I do." When I asked how he pulled that off, he grinned and said, "That's where you come in." We both laughed, and I agreed to go.

That girl was Jenny.

When we picked her up, she immediately told Isaiah to sit in the backseat and slid into the front with me. Her assertiveness caught my attention right away, and so did her confidence. She was exactly my type, and she would quickly figure that out. Jenny almost immediately struck up a conversation, asking me all kinds of questions about myself, while Isaiah sat in the back, giggling to himself.

As we drove, Jenny suddenly announced that she didn't want to go home anymore. "I'd rather hang out with you guys," she said, looking directly at me. "You cool with that?" I'm sure my face turned red, but I told her I didn't mind. We went back to the mall, where I was shoe shopping before she called.

Jenny grabbed my hand and said she loved shopping and would help me find the perfect pair. She stayed by my side, picking out shoes and telling me which ones looked good and which didn't. With every moment, I found myself more and more drawn to her. She knew she had me hooked.

After I bought the shoes she chose, we headed to the food court. Jenny grabbed my hand again, holding it as we walked. "You know this feels right," she said with a smile. I laughed and asked, "Is this how you flirt?" She didn't answer but instead asked me, "Do you have a girlfriend?"

When I said no, she replied, "Well, I guess you do now."

I laughed shaking my head but loving every minute of it.

And that was how Jenny and I began.

Jenny was unlike any girl I had ever talked to. She was Persian, and I had never even hung out with anyone Persian before. While I had grown up with friends from the Middle East in Antioch, none were from Iran, and Jenny's background was entirely new to me. Despite our different upbringings, she was so easy to get along with, so confident in herself, that being around her felt effortless. I loved every minute of being with her.

Physically, Jenny was 100% my type—everything I found attractive. But her personality? That was something else entirely. She was outgoing and optimistic, with a perspective on life that was not only refreshing but inspiring. Her positivity motivated me to aim higher, experience more, and do more in life. Being with her made me feel like I could achieve anything, and I wanted to.

The more we dated, the more we clicked. Every moment we spent together was fun, and as time passed, I realized I was falling in love with her. She surprisingly told me she loved me first, but I'm certain I felt it before she did. Our love grew deeper than I think either of us expected, and it happened fast.

Jenny was everything I had been looking for and everything I never knew I needed. She came into my life at exactly the right time, pulling me out of a dark place and putting me into full-go mode. She brought me back to myself, and for that, I'll always be thankful.

Jenny and I shared so many great times early in our relationship, and we had plenty of perfect dates. But two moments stand out more than any others—one that brought us closer and one that showed me just how much she meant to me.

The first was a road trip to Orlando with her family. Jenny invited me along, knowing it would be an experience since her family primarily spoke Farsi while I only spoke English. She thought the situation would be hilarious but also wanted me there because they were visiting several water parks, and she knew we'd have fun together.

The trip was certainly memorable. Due to a last-minute cancellation, we ended up in one hotel room with only two beds. Jenny and I had to share a bed with her older nephew and his fiancée—a unique experience, to say the least. I made sure to sleep on the outside edge of the bed, but the awkward situation didn't dampen the trip. Jenny and I had a blast at the water parks, and her family's warm and welcoming nature made me feel at home. That experience brought us all closer, and it drew me and Jenny even closer in the process. I think it made her fall deeper in love with me. As for me, I was already there.

The second moment was much more emotional. We'd had a silly argument, the kind of immature disagreement that feels bigger than it is in the moment. It escalated enough for me to break things off with Jenny before heading to work. She called a friend to take her to her family's house, and I went about my day, but I couldn't shake the feeling that I'd made a terrible mistake.

As I worked, the sadness grew heavier, hitting me harder than I'd ever felt before. By the time a coworker mentioned the pouring rain outside, I couldn't take it anymore. I clocked out mid-shift, telling her I had an emergency. Without thinking, I jumped in my car and drove straight to Jenny's house.

When I pulled up, the Coldplay song Talk was playing on a burned CD in my car. The lyrics seemed to match exactly how I felt. I ran to the door, soaked from the rain, and knocked. Her older sister, who she referred to as "Mom," answered with a puzzled look. I asked if I could speak to Jenny. After a moment, her sister came back and said Jenny didn't want to talk.

I refused to leave. "I just need to apologize," I said.

Her sister smiled and disappeared again. When Jenny came to the door, she looked irritated, asking what I was doing there. Standing in the rain, I poured my heart out. I told her how much I regretted what I'd said and how much I loved her. I told her I missed her in the short time we'd been apart and that I never wanted to feel that way again.

Her face softened, and tears welled in her eyes. Before I could say more, she stepped into the rain, grabbed me, and held me tightly. "I love you," she said, "but don't ever let this happen again." I promised her I wouldn't.

To this day, it breaks my heart that I broke that promise.

As mine and Jenny's relationship grew stronger, so did the pressure on us to figure out our next steps. Neither of us made enough money to move out, and neither of us had the experience to navigate adulthood independently. Jenny was stuck in limbo at her family's house, where their expectations for her didn't align with the expectations she had for herself—including being with me.

At the same time, I could feel the pressure building at my sister and brother-in-law's house. Their growing family needed more space, and it was becoming clear that space didn't include me. Instead of going on dates like we used to, Jenny and I spent our time searching for jobs or places to live, but we faced rejection at every turn.

Things eventually boiled over at Jenny's house. Her family gave her an ultimatum, though she never fully shared the details with me. I knew enough to understand that I was on one side of it. Jenny chose me, and as a result, she was told to leave.

Without a place of my own, we scrambled to find her a roommate. We came close a couple of times, but something always fell through. Jenny was devastated and terrified, and I didn't have any answers. Then, out of nowhere, my sister stepped in to save the day.

During a conversation about everything we were going through, she offered to let Jenny move in with us. Their family was already growing, and they didn't have much extra space, but my sister and brother-in-law understood the circumstances and offered to help.

Their generosity blew me away, and I'll always be grateful for the support they gave me and Jenny during those early years of figuring out adulthood.

Jenny and I were surprised but ecstatic. Not only did this solve her immediate problem, but it also brought us closer together. Living under the same roof, even temporarily, gave us a head start on learning how to live with each other. Jenny moved in, and I fell even more in love with her. I loved having her there to kiss me goodbye when I left for work and welcome me home when I returned.

We worked tirelessly to save for a deposit and find a place of our own, but as the deadline approached, the rejections kept piling up. I was running out of options and didn't know what we were going to do.

Then, my cousin Ronnie back in Tennessee reached out. He explained that he was going through a separation and needed a roommate to help with rent. At first, I was hesitant to leave Jenny, but Ronnie made it clear he wasn't open to having both of us there.

I sat on the idea for two days, devastated and unsure of what to do. Finally, I told Jenny we needed to talk. I explained the situation and told her I thought it was best for her to work things out with her family while I moved to Tennessee. We'd exercised every option and it felt like we had no other choice.

Jenny looked me in the eyes, grabbed my hands, and said, "You're not going to Tennessee without me; we'll just have to figure it out."

Her words hit me hard. I called Ronnie and told him I appreciated the offer, but I couldn't come unless Jenny could come too. After some time to think it over with reluctance, he agreed, and just like that, we had a plan.

Although we were relieved to finally have a solution, I wasn't very happy about coming back to Tennessee. It felt like returning to a place I had fought so hard to leave, and I couldn't help but feel like I was taking a step backward. But Jenny was optimistic and positive about the move. She kept reminding me that I wasn't going back alone—that I had her by my side—and that made all the difference.

The move back to Tennessee was bittersweet. If it's possible to feel happy and sad at the same time, that's exactly how I felt. I was thrilled that Jenny was coming with me, but the thought of returning to Tennessee weighed heavily on me. I had never wanted to live there again, and having to go back felt like the ultimate failure.

Jenny, as always, made things easier. She helped me pack, consolidate, and keep my mind off the negatives. She focused on the positives, and her optimism was contagious. On the drive back, I couldn't help but notice the cold air and the gray landscape I had left behind. I remember stopping at a gas station, looking around at the dreariness, and sarcastically telling myself, "Welcome back, Keith."

For Jenny, though, it was a different story. She had never been to Tennessee, and she was excited about the move. She loved the beach but hated Florida's weather and looked forward to experiencing Nashville's seasons. Her enthusiasm brought a smile to my face and made the transition much more bearable.

Moving into Ronnie's apartment turned out to be smoother than I expected. I hadn't been around my cousin in years and didn't know what to anticipate, but I was relieved to find that he was clean, organized, and had a nice place. The area in Hermitage was convenient, and even though I had to sell my car to make the move, I knew I could walk to find work. That alone was a huge relief.

News of my return spread quickly among family members. My aunt was around during the move later sharing the news with other family, and everyone welcomed both Jenny and me with open arms. I found a job relatively quickly at White Castle, which was within walking distance. Shortly after, my grandfather struck a deal with me to buy his 1985 Oldsmobile Delta 88 Royale for $800. That car became iconic among those who knew me back then and served me and Jenny well for years. I'll always be grateful to my papa for that car.

With transportation secured, Jenny found work quickly, picking up waitressing jobs at multiple places. Jenny loved working because she loved making money—and spending it. She was incredibly generous, always buying gifts or finding ways to make our time together special.

I had no problem with her spending her money however she wanted. I took care of our bills and necessities while she used her earnings for anything else we wanted or just for fun. I never wanted Jenny to feel the stress of work. If she ever wanted to quit and stay home, I made sure she knew that she could.

Together, we began building a life in Tennessee—a life that, despite my reservations about returning, started to feel like the beginning of something good.

Although the move to Tennessee was smoother than we anticipated, the transition into daily life brought challenges we hadn't expected. With both of us working, our schedules often clashed, and Ronnie's visitation with his son sometimes created additional conflicts. Finding time for ourselves while managing separate schedules and sharing a living space with a roommate required patience and flexibility.

The adjustment wasn't easy, but we kept our focus on the positives—something Jenny's optimistic personality made possible. We celebrated the small wins, like buying our first pieces of furniture, a television, and a blow-up mattress.

We dressed that mattress up like a real bed, only to wake up halfway sunk to the floor in the mornings. When we finally bought a proper bed, it felt like a huge victory, and we celebrated accordingly.

Financially, things started to look up. I received a promotion, and Jenny picked up a second job. Together, we were able to buy her first car—a white Ford Taurus. She loved that car and was so proud of it. I was proud of us for getting to that point. With two cars, promising incomes, and more experience under our belts, life felt like it was on the upswing.

But as time went on, things began to clash with Ronnie. Like most roommate situations, tensions eventually surfaced, and it became clear that we were approaching the next stage of our journey—one that we hoped we were ready for.

When Jenny and I finally came to terms with the fact that we needed to move and get our own place, the pressure was on. We couldn't help but feel some initial discouragement, remembering the struggles we faced in Florida. But this time, things were different. We had experience, credit, and two steady incomes. That reality hadn't fully hit us until we started looking.

The first place we checked was Spinnaker Cove, located right across the street from Ronnie's apartment. I spoke with the leasing agent without any real expectation of being approved, but during that same interview, they ran our credit and application—and we were approved on the spot.

I'll never forget the feeling of touring that apartment. It was on the third floor, overlooking the pool, and everything about it felt perfect. It was close to everything we knew but entirely ours. For the first time, it felt like we had endless possibilities ahead of us. Two young kids with two cars, two decent incomes, and a place to call our own—it was pure bliss.

Once we confirmed the move, we spoke with Ronnie. While the timing wasn't ideal for anyone, he understood, and we worked out the details before moving out shortly after.

Our first night in the apartment was simple but unforgettable. We didn't have much beyond the furniture we'd used in our room at Ronnie's, so we ordered pizza and sat on the living room floor, going over plans for our new place. It was the best feeling in the world and a memory I'll cherish forever.

CHAPTER 3

BUILDING A LIFE TOGETHER

L iving in our first apartment together felt like a dream. Those early days were full of excitement as Jenny and I worked during the day and spent our evenings shopping for things to make the apartment our own. Buying our first living room set was a proud moment. I'll never forget sitting on the sofa for the first time, looking around at the room we had arranged just the way we wanted. We smiled at each other, knowing this was a milestone in the life we were building together.

Once the apartment was furnished, life settled into a comforting routine. We'd lounge on the couch with our cat, Kiki, spending quiet nights watching movies and TV shows. It felt good to have a place to call our own. As the honeymoon phase wore off, we started venturing out more, exploring Nashville together. We made it our mission to try every restaurant, shop at every store, and visit every corner of the city, capturing memories for our Myspace pages along the way.

Introducing Jenny to my friends and family was another special part of this time. Her outgoing personality made it easy for everyone to love her. She wasn't just kind; she genuinely wanted to connect with the people who mattered to me. My friends enjoyed her company, and my family welcomed her with open arms. She even joined me and my friends at Titans and Predators games, eager to learn about the sports that were such a big part of my life. Jenny's willingness to embrace everything I loved made me appreciate her even more.

For the first couple of years, things between us were almost perfect. We were so in sync that challenges seemed nonexistent. Our personalities complemented each other, and we were both clean, organized people who shared a similar schedule and many of the same interests. That harmony carried us for a long time, keeping our relationship strong and steady.

But as time went on, we grew more comfortable in our relationship, and our focus began to shift outward.

We started spending time with friends outside of the relationship, which eventually led to episodes of jealousy. My friends would sometimes want to hang out with just me, and Jenny's coworkers would occasionally invite her out, and these moments of separation began to create tension.

At first, we avoided confronting these feelings, thinking it would prevent arguments. But holding things inside only made matters worse. Over time, small frustrations built up, and when they finally boiled over, minor disagreements would escalate into major conflicts. These fights, born out of issues we'd avoided for too long, became harder to control. Eventually, one of these arguments would lead to our first breakup. Jenny moved back to Florida with her family, and for the first time, our relationship felt truly shaken.

The breakup left me broken-hearted on a level I had never experienced before. But it wasn't just the loss of Jenny that hit me—it was the realization that, for the first time in my life, I was completely on my own. I was an adult navigating life alone, and the weight of processing both the heartbreak and the solitude was overwhelming. It felt like everything I had built was suddenly gone, and I was left trying to figure out how to move forward.

The adrenaline of standing firm during our final argument lasted for the first couple of days. But after that, the reality of her absence set in. Being in the apartment alone felt suffocating, like the walls were closing in around me. Everywhere I went in the city, every corner of our home, memories of Jenny swirled, overwhelming me. I couldn't escape the reminders of her. I leaned on my friends and family, pouring out my feelings to anyone willing to listen. There were moments I couldn't stop talking about her, and sometimes I'd cry openly to those I trusted most. I couldn't watch TV or movies or even listen to music without thinking of her. The weight of losing her, combined with being on my own for the first time, was crushing.

I turned to smoking more heavily to cope. I lost weight from a lack of appetite and ate only because I knew I had to. Drinking water felt like the only easy task I could maintain. Over time, I found some relief in spending time with my friends, creating new memories unconnected to Jenny. For a while, it seemed like I was starting to heal. During that time, I wrote multiple songs about Jenny and the breakup. Music became my outlet, and I poured all my emotions into the lyrics. I would post the songs on Myspace, hoping Jenny might see them. Sometimes, I'd notice subtle responses on her page-just enough to give me a glimmer of hope before it faded away again. This back-and-forth motivated me to write even more, and for the first time, I started taking writing seriously. These songs mattered in a way nothing else had before because I wanted her to know exactly how I felt.

Then one night, while hanging out with Julian, I checked Jenny's Myspace profile and saw her updated profile picture. She wasn't alone. She had a new boyfriend. My progress crumbled beneath me. Julian tried to reassure me, suggesting it might be a family member or a friend, but I knew better. Jenny had moved on. I was devastated, but Julian did what he always did best-he made me laugh. He joked about the guy, making fun of him to lighten the mood. His humor worked, and I joined in. That night, Julian and I did something immature and reckless to cheer ourselves up. He suggested we mess with the guy. My better judgment told me not to, but I wasn't in the mood for better judgment.

Julian's plan was bold: leave an embarrassing photo of himself-a full-body shot from behind-on the guy's Myspace wall. It wasn't just a casual picture; it was Julian, completely naked from behind, showing off his bare butt in all its glory. At first, I hesitated, but when the guy sent me a message boasting about "taking my girl," flaunting his money, and bragging about his car, I told Julian to do it. Within minutes of the photo going live, chaos ensued. The guy's comment section lit up with people asking why there was a naked butt on his page. Friends, strangers, and mutual connections were all chiming in, creating a hilarious back-and-forth. The guy frantically responded in all caps, begging Julian to take it down: "WHAT IS THIS?? DELETE THIS NOW!!!"

Julian and I couldn't breathe from laughing so hard. Every new comment only made it funnier. Some people were horrified, others were crying-laughing, and a few seemed genuinely confused, asking, "Dude, why is this on your page?" Then Jenny responded. Her comment read: "Julian, take it down lol." That "lol" was all I needed to see. It gave me hope. It showed me she thought it was funny, and that maybe-not entirely-I wasn't lost to her. It was in that moment I knew I needed to fix this. needed to get my girl back.

The "lol" in Jenny's comment felt like a shot of adrenaline to my confidence. For months, I had been lost in the darkness of her absence, but that one light-hearted reaction brought back a spark I hadn't felt in so long. I regained an energy I hadn't had since she left, and I channeled it into writing new music. My songs became more personal, more raw, and I posted them on Myspace, hoping she would hear them.

Eventually, she did. Jenny reached out to me in a message, saying she wanted to talk. During our conversations, she mentioned hearing my new songs and complimented how much my writing had improved. She told me she was proud that I was continuing to write and record and that she was glad I hadn't given up on music. Always quick with a joke, she teased that maybe we should break up more often if it meant pulling that level of talent out of me.

As we talked, we laid everything out on the table. I opened up about how I'd been feeling during the months she was gone—the loneliness, the heartbreak, and how much I missed her. She admitted that things hadn't been much better for her in Florida. We both apologized for the mistakes we'd made, acknowledged how much we missed each other, and agreed to put the past behind us.

With a sense of renewed hope, Jenny decided to come back home.

When Jenny came back to Tennessee after our reconciliation, it felt like a fresh start—a second chance to build something stronger. We both knew this time had to be different. The breakup had been a wake-up call, teaching us just how fragile things could be without trust. We tackled the jealousy and insecurities head-on, promising to be more honest and open with each other.

Life after she returned had a renewed energy. We didn't want to fall back into old habits, so we put more effort into making the most of our time together. Between our full-time jobs, it wasn't always easy to connect, but we made it a priority. Trips became our way of escaping the daily grind and rediscovering the joy in each other's company. One of the best trips was to Gatlinburg with a close friend of mine and his girlfriend. We visited Dollywood, rode go karts in Pigeon Forge and even bungee-jumped spending the weekend laughing and letting go of the past. It was a reminder of everything we loved about being together.

Jenny's older sister also came to visit during this time, and it was a meaningful moment for both of us. Their bond was unshakable—they had leaned on each other through so much, especially after losing their mother. Seeing Jenny with her sister gave me a deeper appreciation for her family and the strength they shared. Her sister's visit reminded me that our relationship wasn't just about us; it was about the lives and families we were blending together.

During her sister's visit, we spent an afternoon at the Opryland Hotel. It was a beautiful day, and we wandered through the lush gardens, taking in the atmosphere. At one point, Jenny led me to an altar in the garden and grabbed my hands. She smiled and said, "This feels right, doesn't it?" I looked at her, caught up in the moment, and smiled back. "I think I've heard this before." I replied smiling, "Yes, it does." Jenny's smile widened, and then she asked, "So when are you going to ask me to marry you?"

I was caught off guard. Her question hung in the air, and I quickly answered, "When the timing is right." She didn't hesitate, replying, "Well, I'm ready to be Mrs. Norfleet, so..." Before I could say anything else, her sister called us over, breaking the moment.

It was the first time Jenny had brought up marriage, and I knew she was serious. That made me nervous. It wasn't that I didn't want to marry her—I just didn't feel ready. Financially, emotionally, and even logistically, it felt like too much to take on at that moment. But hearing her say those words stayed with me. It was clear that she saw a future for us, and while I wasn't sure how to approach it then, I knew it was something I had to think about.

Back at home, life found its rhythm. Jenny was thriving at work and loved the independence of earning her own money. She'd often surprise me with gifts or thoughtful gestures that showed how much she cared. I made it my responsibility to handle the bills and other essentials because I wanted her to feel free to focus on what made her happy. I also made it clear she didn't have to keep working if it ever became too much.

The biggest shift came in how we approached our relationship. We stopped sweating the small stuff and learned to let go of petty arguments. Jealousy became less of an issue as trust grew stronger. We reminded ourselves constantly that we were a team, and that made all the difference. I also worked on being more patient and listening better—things I knew I had struggled with before.

Looking back, that time felt like real growth for both of us. It wasn't perfect, but we were committed to making it work. Having Jenny back was a gift, and I wasn't going to take it for granted. Together, we focused on creating a life where we could thrive—not just as a couple, but as individuals who supported each other every step of the way.

Looking back, that time in our relationship taught me so much about love, trust, and communication. Jenny's return felt like a second chance, and it made me realize how fragile relationships can be without intentional effort. The breakup had forced me to confront my own flaws—my impatience, my tendency to hold things in until they boiled over, and my struggles with jealousy. Rebuilding our relationship gave me a new perspective on what it meant to truly be there for someone you love.

At the same time, the question of marriage lingered in my mind. Jenny's comment at the Opryland Hotel—"When are you going to ask me to marry you?"—had left an impression I couldn't shake. I knew she was serious, and I knew she saw me as her future. That thought was both exciting and terrifying.

The truth was, I didn't feel ready. Marriage felt like such a monumental step, and I wasn't sure if I could give her everything she deserved. Financially, I didn't think I was in the right place. Emotionally, I wasn't sure if I could handle the weight of such a commitment. And deep down, I was afraid of failing her. I loved Jenny with everything I had, but the idea of making that kind of promise and not living up to it scared me.

Instead of sharing these fears, I kept them to myself. I convinced myself that waiting for the "right time" was the best choice. But looking back, I wonder if I underestimated how much she valued the love we already shared. Maybe she wasn't looking for perfection—maybe she just wanted us to take that next step together, flaws and all.

Those reflections stayed with me, shaping how I approached our relationship moving forward. They made me realize how much I valued Jenny and how much I wanted our life together to succeed. And while I didn't have all the answers then, I knew one thing for certain: Jenny was the person I wanted to share my life with.

This phase of our relationship taught me that love isn't perfect, but it's always worth fighting for if both people are willing to grow. It showed me that redemption is possible, even after mistakes, as long as there's honesty and a willingness to change. I learned that love isn't just about the big, dramatic gestures—it's in the small, consistent acts of care and understanding. Jenny and I didn't just rebuild our relationship; we redefined it, making it more resilient and meaningful.

In many ways, this chapter prepared me for the challenges that lay ahead. It taught me that life is unpredictable and that love requires adaptability and patience. It showed me the value of forgiveness—not just forgiving each other, but forgiving ourselves for past mistakes. This period in our lives reminded me that even when things fall apart, there's always a chance to start over if you're willing to put in the work.

Looking back, this was one of the most transformative phases of my life. It wasn't always easy, but it was real, and it was ours. It taught me that love isn't just about being together; it's about growing together. And while I didn't know it at the time, those lessons would carry me through the joys and heartbreaks that were yet to come.

CHAPTER 4

BREAK UP, TO MAKE UP

Rebuilding trust after our initial breakup was not easy, and while Jenny and I made progress, insecurities lingered beneath the surface. These insecurities were exacerbated by the situations we found ourselves in, particularly as we began spending time with others outside our relationship. Jealousy wasn't constant, but when it did arise, it added strain to our bond and made it harder to fully rebuild what we had lost.

One of the biggest challenges we faced was the influence of outside voices. Many of Jenny's friends were single and encouraged her to go out more, often to clubs and bars—something she hadn't done much before. These outings introduced her to a lifestyle of heavy drinking and partying that was completely new for her. At the same time, I had people in my ear—some single, others with their own biases—who encouraged me to walk away from Jenny. They claimed her new social life was incompatible with the stable relationship I wanted. Being young and inexperienced, we didn't have the tools to manage these pressures effectively, and the presence of so many outside opinions made it difficult for us to navigate this portion of our relationship.

Jenny's newfound social life brought excitement and freedom for her, but it also introduced risks and challenges. As she spent more time with her single friends, she was often surrounded by people who didn't have our relationship's best interests at heart. Many of these nights out involved other men attempting to insert themselves into our relationship, creating situations that heightened my insecurities. While I trusted Jenny, the constant interference made it harder to maintain that trust without conflict.

Both of us were working full-time, which left limited time to reconnect and focus on each other. This lack of consistent quality time allowed the influence of friends and social circles to grow stronger. The more time Jenny spent out with her friends, the more isolated I felt. Similarly, my time spent with people who weren't invested in our success as a couple reinforced doubts and frustrations, creating a cycle that was hard to break.

Our differing perspectives on marriage also became a growing challenge. Jenny saw marriage as the natural next step in our relationship and was ready for that commitment. I, however, was hesitant. My fears about financial readiness, emotional preparedness, and my ability to meet her expectations left me feeling stuck. Instead of openly sharing these fears, I kept them to myself, hoping that waiting for the "right time" would resolve the issue. In hindsight, I feel my silence may have unintentionally made Jenny feel undervalued or uncertain about our future together.

While we tried to improve our communication after reconciling, certain topics—like her growing social life or my hesitations about marriage—remained difficult to discuss. Rather than addressing these issues head-on, we often avoided them, thinking it would prevent arguments. Unfortunately, this avoidance allowed tensions to build, creating a rift that became harder to close.

Even though we had reconciled, the pain and insecurities from our initial breakup still lingered. These unresolved feelings influenced our interactions in subtle ways, making it harder to fully move forward as a couple. While we both wanted to leave the past behind, its shadow often crept into our present, creating emotional distance. The connection that had once felt unbreakable began to weaken under the weight of these unresolved issues.

Our final breakup wasn't the result of one single incident but rather the culmination of all these challenges. One night, during a heated argument, I had reached a breaking point. I gave Jenny an ultimatum: if she went out with her friends that night, it would mean the end of our relationship. She chuckled at my words and said "I'll see you in the morning." not taking a word I'd said seriously. When she left anyway, I felt like I had no choice but to follow through. The next morning, when she tried to reconcile, I reminded her of my ultimatum and told her we were done.

What neither of us expected was the turmoil that would follow. Although we had broken up, we were forced to continue living together in the same apartment. Suddenly, the space we had built together as a couple became a constant reminder of what we had lost. Navigating this new reality—living single but sharing the same space—was one of the most difficult periods of my life. The emotional weight of our breakup and the strain of seeing each other every day while trying to move on created a tension that was impossible to escape.

Living together after the breakup was an incredibly complex and emotionally draining experience, filled with tension, regret, and moments of outright conflict. Our relationship had already reached a fragile point before the breakup, and being forced to coexist under the same roof amplified the intensity of everything we were feeling. What had once been a loving relationship became a battlefield of jealousy, frustration, and immaturity.

Emotionally, I was torn apart. Seeing Jenny every day was a constant reminder of what no longer was, but it also kept hope alive that we might somehow find a way back to each other. At the same time, jealousy and insecurity consumed me as I watched her begin to reclaim her independence in ways that often felt like she was intentionally pushing me away. I found myself struggling to balance my lingering love for her with the pain of knowing we were no longer together. The emotional rollercoaster was exhausting. One moment, I felt guilty for my own role in the breakup; the next, I was angry at her for seemingly moving on so quickly. My mind was constantly racing, replaying our arguments and trying to figure out what I could have done differently to prevent us from reaching this point.

Daily life became a minefield. Simple tasks like eating or watching TV often turned into moments of awkward silence or subtle jabs at one another. While we tried to maintain a level of civility, the unspoken tension was palpable. There were days when we didn't speak at all, retreating to our own corners of the apartment just to avoid confrontation. The jealousy between us escalated during this time. Being young, inexperienced, and immature, we both began playing games to intentionally make the other jealous. It started small—comments about new friendships or exaggerated stories about how much fun we were having apart—but it quickly spiraled into something far more damaging. For me, it was a way to regain control in a situation where I felt powerless. For Jenny, it seemed like a way to prove she could move on without me.

The jealousy game took on a life of its own. Jenny, encouraged by her single friends, began going out to clubs and bars more frequently, drinking heavily, and immersing herself in a social scene she had never been a part of before. These outings led to more attention from other men, which she didn't shy away from flaunting. While at work at Dave & Buster's—a hot spot for big names in Nashville—Jenny was introduced to several players from the Tennessee Titans and eventually Steve McNair. What began as an attempt to make me jealous quickly escalated. Jenny started dating some of the Titans players she'd met, and she didn't hesitate to let me know about it. The more I pursued other women, the more Jenny flaunted her relationships in front of me. Her actions were intentional, calculated to hurt me as much as possible because she was hurting, and they succeeded.

At the same time, I wasn't innocent in this situation. My pursuit of my sister's friend, encouraged by my sister herself, created a heated rivalry between Jenny, my sister, and her best friend. This rivalry only fueled Jenny's determination to take her actions to the next level. What started as a game of jealousy between the two of us turned into an all-out emotional war, with both of us trying to outdo the other in ways that ultimately caused more harm than either of us anticipated.

Our interactions during this time were strained at best and hostile at worst. On the surface, we tried to maintain some level of respect for one another, but underneath, the resentment and anger were impossible to ignore. When we did speak, it often turned into an argument, with both of us throwing verbal jabs fueled by our jealousy and hurt. Jenny's behavior—her nights out, her new relationships, and her increasingly bold efforts to flaunt them—left me feeling humiliated and betrayed. At the same time, I knew my actions weren't helping. My involvement with my sister's friend only escalated the situation, creating a cycle of retaliation that neither of us seemed willing to break.

Despite all of this, there were moments when the weight of what we were doing hit me. I'd see Jenny come home after a night out, looking tired or upset, and I'd wonder if she was as hurt by all of this as I was. But neither of us knew how to stop. We were too caught up in the game, too focused on winning whatever battle we thought we were fighting, to see the damage we were causing to ourselves and each other.

This period of living together after the breakup was a turning point for me. It forced me to confront my own immaturity and the ways I had contributed to the toxic dynamic between us. I realized how much of my behavior was driven by fear—fear of losing Jenny, fear of being alone, and fear of admitting my own faults. At the same time, it showed me how powerful jealousy can be, not just as an emotion but as a destructive force. The choices we made during this time—whether it was Jenny dating other men or me seeing other women—were reactions to that jealousy, and they only pushed us further apart.

Despite everything we had been through—our efforts to make each other jealous, the new people in our lives, and even the knowledge that Jenny had dated Titans players—

there was somehow still a lingering thread of hope between us. Living together as exes had been chaotic, but neither of us had entirely closed the door on the possibility of reconciliation. That door opened one last time when Jenny approached me about the Hawaii trip we had planned earlier in the year.

The trip, booked during better times, had become a bittersweet symbol of our relationship. In a moment of weakness, let her guard down. She suggested we still go, not just to avoid wasting the money but to use the trip as an opportunity to determine if there was anything left to salvage between us. She told me the relationship deserved the respect of one final attempt to figure things out. As heartwarming as it was to hear I was hesitant. Every possibility ran through my mind during the days I spent mulling it over, but ultimately, I agreed. Deep down, I still loved Jenny, and despite everything, I wanted to see if we could find our way back to each other.

We promised to leave the chaos and jealousy behind and focus on us. Jenny even ended things with a new guy she had been seeing regularly, and I let my sister's friend know that I needed space to see if see if mending our relationship was possible. Neither of them were happy about it, but it didn't matter to us at the time. This trip was going to be about me and Jenny—no one else.

The trip started with optimism and excitement. We immersed ourselves in every excursion, from jungle hikes to waterfalls to a nighttime spectacle where we watched a live volcano erupting in the ocean. I'll never forget holding Jenny in my arms on the ship's deck, the lava shooting into the sky and sizzling as it hit the water. It was one of the most awe-inspiring moments of my life, and for that brief time, it felt like we had rediscovered what made us fall in love in the first place.

By day, we were two people in love again, laughing, exploring, and enjoying the beauty of Hawaii. By night, however, everything shifted. Our emotions would rise to the surface, and the conversations we needed to have could no longer be avoided. Those discussions were raw and unfiltered, often leading to arguments instead of resolutions. Jealousy and pain from the past months kept bubbling up, overshadowing the progress we were trying to make. Despite the emotional roller coaster, every argument ended the same way: with us in each other's arms by the end of the night, holding on to what little hope we had left.

The last night of the trip, things seemed to turn a corner. Jenny told me she was ready to give us another try if I was. She said that no matter what had happened, it didn't compare to how much I meant to her. Hearing those words lifted a weight off my shoulders, and I told her I felt the same. We agreed to make it official when we got home.

On the flight back, Jenny brought up an idea. She said we should write down questions for each other—hard questions that needed honest answers—before we started over. She wanted everything out in the open to make sure there were no lingering doubts or secrets. We scribbled our questions on a piece of scrap paper, answering them one by one. The conversation was difficult but cathartic, and it felt like we were finally building a foundation for a fresh start.

Then came the last question.

Jenny asked me,

"Do you have feelings for her?"

I paused, trying to find the right words. I wanted to be honest, but I also didn't want to ruin the progress we had made. Finally, I admitted

"I was beginning to."

Jenny's face fell, but she stayed composed as she asked one final question:

"Do you love her?"

I hesitated, unsure of how to answer. I didn't want to lie, but I also didn't know the truth myself. Finally, I said,

"I don't know."

The look on Jenny's face will stay with me forever. It wasn't anger or frustration—it was pure, undeniable heartbreak. My vague answer was enough to shatter everything we had rebuilt on that trip. Jenny looked at me and said, "This conversation is over, we are over. When we get home, I'm packing my things and moving out."

I was devastated, at a loss for words and so disappointed in myself for being so stupid to say those things in that moment but for Jenny there was nothing left to be said. That was the longest, coldest and most quiet flight home I've ever been on.

When we returned, things quickly grew more complicated. Shortly after we got back, Jenny shocked me with the news she was pregnant. She handed me the test and said, without a doubt, that the child was mine. The news brought a wave of even more conflicting emotions. Part of me wanted to forget everything that had happened, beg her to put it all behind us and fully commit to Jenny and the baby if she'd let me. Another part, however, was consumed by the doubts others had planted in my mind. People whispered that the baby might not even be mine, and although I knew Jenny had always been honest with me, I allowed their chatter to creep into my thoughts.

When I asked Jenny if the baby might not be mine, the pain in her eyes was unmistakable. She didn't yell or argue; she simply said, "You'll never have to fight to be in your child's life, but we're figuring this out separately." That marked the end of the idea of reconciliation. The relationship we had tried so hard to rebuild crumbled under the weight of everything we had gone through.

About a month later, Jenny would tell me she suffered a miscarriage further adding to the whirlwind of unfamiliar emotions. She provided proof from the doctor, and it confirmed what she said. We had gone to the same doctor earlier, who had confirmed the pregnancy, so I had no reason to doubt her. The loss, which the doctor attributed to stress, hit us both hard. As hard as I was taking it all, I can't even imagine the emotional weight Jenny carried during that time.

Shortly after the miscarriage, Jenny moved out. She stayed true to her word, packing her things and moving in with her friend from work at an apartment complex called Cherry Creek. That move marked the official and final end of our relationship.

The final breakup hit me harder than ever before. Everything I had dealt with during our first breakup came rushing back with even more force. I fell back into old habits, smoking heavily and now pairing it with drinking in an attempt to drown the pain. All the preparation I had built up during the months apart was undone by the hope we had rekindled during our near reconciliation in Hawaii. The abrupt reversal at the end left me blindsided, struggling to find a way to cope.

I leaned on friends and family, but just like before, it provided only temporary relief. I hated feeling like a burden and taking up their time with my problems. However, I remembered what had helped me heal during our first breakup and quickly turned back to music. My closest friend, Joe, was a huge part of this process. We worked together at White Castle and shared a deep passion for writing and recording music. Together, we created some of the best music I've ever been a part of. Joe was there for me through every phase of that time in my life, whether we were recording, hanging out, or just talking things out. Having someone who knew both me and Jenny helped, as he understood the situation on a deeper level.

At the same time, I realized I needed to address my relationship with my sister's friend. The emotions I was juggling were too conflicting, and I knew it wasn't fair to her or to myself to continue as we had been. I sent her an email, explaining that I didn't think it was wise for us to keep talking. I told her I needed to focus on myself and sort out my feelings. I also admitted that even though Jenny and I weren't together and I had no idea where things would go, I was still in love with her. Pursuing something with her while my heart was still tied to Jenny didn't feel right. I never received a response, so I moved forward, redirecting my focus inward.

This time, I pushed myself to do things differently. I forced myself to get out of the house, work out, and eat healthier. While the pain was immense, I channeled every ounce of energy I had into fighting through it. On the positive side, I was learning to handle heartbreak in a more constructive way. On the negative side, I was growing addicted to going out and drinking. What started as weekend outings turned into multiple nights a week at clubs and bars. It became a distraction, a way to mask the pain. I started linking up with any girl who caught my attention, recklessly chasing fleeting connections to fill the void Jenny had left.

Meanwhile, it became clear that Jenny was still paying attention. She would pop up unexpectedly, playfully flirting whenever she did. It was obvious there was still something between us, but the damage we had inflicted on each other was immense, and neither of us knew how to begin to fix it. One day, while I was on a break at work, Jenny showed up in a brand-new Escalade. I had no idea why, but I played it cool. She walked up with her hair and makeup done, wearing an outfit she knew I liked, and smelling like the perfume I had bought her for her birthday. She sat on my lap, smiling mischievously.

"You got a girlfriend yet?" she asked with a smile.

I smirked and replied sarcastically, "I don't know."

She didn't like that answer.

"Well, I just wanted to swing by and see how you were doing," she said.

"Oh yeah?" I asked.

"Yeah, I've been missing you a little," she teased, holding up her fingers to indicate "just a tiny bit" with a playful smirk.

I laughed smiling back at her as she walked back to her truck, knowing exactly how to stay in my head. I could tell that I was still in hers, too. Moments like these fueled my creativity, and I threw myself even deeper into music, committing to finally making an album.

Then, everything changed during a recording session with Vince, the father of Jenny's best friend's child. As we worked, Vince brought up Jenny.

"I can't believe how everything changed with you two," he said. "It's crazy who she's talking to now."

Confused, I asked, "What do you mean? Who is she talking to?"

"You haven't heard? You haven't seen the Escalade?" he asked.

"Yeah, I saw the truck, but what about it?"

"You think she can afford that truck?" he said with a laugh.

"Who is it?" I asked again.

"Steve McNair, bro. Jenny is seriously dating Steve McNair, Kayla told me all about it."

At first, I thought he was joking. McNair was my favorite NFL player of all time.

"Are you serious?" I asked.

"Yes, bro. They met at her job, and she's been talking to him for a while since she moved out."

I sat there in silence, trying to process what he was saying. Vince added, "Kayla said she couldn't believe Jenny would do that, knowing how much you liked him as a football player."

Reality hit me like a ton of bricks. Not only had Jenny moved on, but she was now dating Steve McNair? It was a surreal and devastating realization. The woman I had loved was now with the man I had idolized as a kid, and the weight of that truth was almost too much to bear.

Shock. That was the only word to describe how I felt when I first learned Jenny was dating Steve McNair. At first, I couldn't process it. The news seemed surreal, like something that could only happen in a movie or on TV. I felt nothing—not because I didn't care, but because my mind simply couldn't comprehend it. For a while, I half-convinced myself it wasn't real. But as the signs started to pile up, reality began to sink in, and with it came an avalanche of thoughts and emotions I wasn't equipped to handle.

The memories of me and Jenny—the life we'd built together—were suddenly overshadowed by new images in my mind of her with McNair, the football player I had looked up to for years. It was excruciating. I talked to everyone I trusted, searching for advice or insight, but even they struggled to make sense of the situation. Why me? How in the world could this possibly happen? It felt like the universe was playing a cruel joke, one I couldn't escape.

Looking back now, I realize my own actions possibly contributed to Jenny's decision. My clubbing, chasing other women, and a brief on-again, off-again relationship with a girl named Katie that Jenny eventually saw me with, likely influenced her to go in that direction. Jenny had options—she always did. McNair wasn't even the first Tennessee Titans player she had dated. But something about her decision to call McNair back seemed different, it felt personal.

The clues started to add up when coworkers told me Jenny had shown up at my job on my day off—with McNair. Hearing that felt like a punch to the gut. Luckily, I wasn't there to see it, but moves like that made it clear Jenny was still playing the game, only this time with much higher stakes. To this day, I can't say for certain what drove her to pursue him, but I have my suspicions. Perhaps it started as a reaction to my behavior, a way to make me feel what she had felt. Or maybe it was something more—something I'll never fully understand. What I do know is that her actions cut deeper than I ever thought possible, because despite everything, I was still in love with her.

As time went by and the reality of them dating started to set in, I thankfully and gradually began finding a bit of normalcy again. I picked up where I left off, trying to shake all the negative thoughts while focusing on myself and improving in any way I knew how. I poured my emotions into music and writing again, finishing two songs I had started about Jenny and everything that had transpired. These tracks were some of my most heartfelt work, and after mastering them, I uploaded them to MySpace, SoundClick, and Reverb. The reception was overwhelmingly positive, but for me, the experience was bittersweet—a reminder of what I had lost and a feeling of "too little, too late."

A couple of nights after posting the songs, I was outside on my balcony smoking a cigarette, lost in thought. Suddenly, I heard music blaring from a car entering the complex. At first, I didn't think much of it, but as the vehicle drew closer, I recognized the song—it was mine. Shocked, I watched as the black SUV parked directly in front of my apartment. Jenny stepped out, her face determined, and before I could process what was happening, she ran up the stairs and knocked on my door.

I opened the door, and there she stood, breathing heavily from running up the stairs. Without hesitation, she jumped into my arms, hugging me tightly. Her presence, her energy—it was all overwhelming. She kissed me passionately, and in that moment, no words were necessary. That kiss held all the emotions of the past year.

When the kiss ended, she looked into my eyes and said, "I love your new songs. Why didn't you write them sooner?" I admitted that I had held myself back because of everything that was going on and I was unsure of how to proceed. She shook her head no and said, "Don't do that anymore. Keep writing." I promised her I would. She smiled and told me she had to go to work but assured me she would call me later.

I was left dumbfounded. Jenny—the woman I still loved, who had been dating my favorite football player of all time—had just shown up at my doorstep playing my song. She kissed me and told me she loved it and I had no idea what to make of it, but I knew it was best not to overthink it. She would eventually call me later and we'd make plans to hang out.

Our conversations would gradually grow more personal as we spent more time together. It wasn't long before Jenny brought up McNair directly. One night, as we sat on her couch, she hesitantly said, "I need to tell you something."

I nodded, sensing the weight of her words.

She began to explain how McNair had pursued her persistently. "At first, I thought it was a joke. I mean, he was there with his family, Keith. His wife and kids were right there, and he still gave me his number." Her voice was a mixture of frustration and regret.

I listened carefully as she detailed how he had returned to her workplace repeatedly, wearing her down with his charm and promises. "He told me he was getting a divorce. That it was over between them," she said, her voice trailing off.

I struggled to keep my emotions in check. "Jenny, do you really believe that? Do you honestly think he was being truthful?"

She hesitated, then shook her head. "I don't know anymore. But at the time, I did. And I let myself believe it because it was easier than facing everything that was going on with us."

Her admission hit me hard, but I remained composed. "Jenny, I don't think you're the only one he's told these things to. Guys like him—guys in his position—they know what to say to keep things going on the side."

She nodded, tears welling up in her eyes. "I know now," she said quietly.

The conversation shifted when she mentioned wanting to tell McNair's wife about their relationship.

"I think she deserves to know," Jenny said firmly.

I immediately shook my head. "Jenny, listen to me. I understand where you're coming from, but this is dangerous. If you tell his wife, she's not going to be mad at him—she's going to be mad at you. And trust me, you don't want to put yourself in that position."

She looked at me, conflicted. "But she deserves to know the truth."

"I get that," I said, leaning forward, "but this isn't the way. You have no idea how this could backfire. People in his world have a lot to lose, and they'll do whatever it takes to protect themselves."

Jenny seemed to take my words to heart. She promised she wouldn't say anything, but deep down, I wasn't convinced.

Despite the emotional heaviness, we continued trying to rebuild our connection. For a while, it felt like we were making progress. But then, the texts started to slow, and the calls became less frequent.

I began to sense something was off. One evening, I sent her a message:

"Jenny, you know I don't want to be an option. If you're still undecided about us and what's going on with him, I'll make it easier for you— just pick him. I can't keep doing this to myself."

I hit send, knowing it might be the end of everything. When days passed without a response, I assumed she had made her choice.

One night, I was sitting in my bedroom talking to Julian, trying to make sense of it all. Julian and I had grown up as die-hard Titans fans. His favorite player was Eddie George, and mine was McNair. We had their jerseys, watched every game, and lived and died by the results of every Sunday. For both of us, this situation felt unreal. Julian knew Jenny well and couldn't believe she would do something like this. As we sat there, dissecting the insanity of it all, my phone rang.

It was Jenny.

I hesitated before picking up, my stomach in knots as I wondered what she could possibly want. Nervously, I answered the call. On the other end, I heard her crying. Instinctively, my protective side kicked in.

"What's wrong?" I asked.

Through her tears, she said she had been pulled over downtown and was being arrested for a DUI. Her voice trembled as she explained that she was going to jail and needed my help.

"Can you please come get my truck for me?" she pleaded. "I don't want them to tow it."

I looked at Julian, who had heard everything on speakerphone. Without hesitation, I grabbed my keys off the desk and told her, "Calm down, I'm on my way."

Julian rode with me, listening to my growing frustration as we headed downtown. I kept replaying her words in my mind, trying to make sense of it all. Why call me? Why not him? The thought of McNair briefly crossed my mind, but I brushed it aside. She's scared—that's all that matters right now, I told myself.

When we arrived at the location Jenny had given me, her truck was nowhere to be seen. We circled the block a couple of times, checking every nearby parking lot and side street, but there was no sign of it. My frustration was growing when finally, I spotted a police officer parked nearby and pulled up next to him. Rolling down my window, I motioned for his attention.

"Excuse me, officer," I began. "My ex-girlfriend called me and said she'd been pulled over for a DUI. She asked me to pick up her truck before it got towed, but I can't seem to find it."

The officer leaned closer, studying me for a moment before responding. "I'm the one who pulled her over," he said, almost casually.

That caught me off guard. "Oh," I said, unsure of what to say next. "Well... is there any way I can get her truck?"

He shook his head and chuckled lightly. "That's not how it works, man. The truck's already been impounded."

Disappointed but not surprised, I asked, "Is she in jail?"

He hesitated. "I can't answer that."

Annoyed, I thanked him and was about to drive away when he stopped me. "Wait, you said you're her boyfriend?"

"Ex," I clarified, my frustration mounting.

The officer nodded slowly, his expression unreadable. "Well, just so you know—she wasn't alone in the truck."

My stomach dropped. "What do you mean?" I asked, feeling a knot tighten in my chest.

He hesitated before answering. "Do you follow football?"

I stared at him, already piecing it together. "Steve McNair?" I asked cautiously, though deep down, I already knew the answer.

The officer gave a knowing look and slowly nodded yes.

I thanked him curtly, rolled up my window, and drove away, my mind swirling with unanswered questions. Julian sat silently beside me, wide-eyed and speechless for the first time all night.

As I drove home, I replayed the entire situation in my mind. The reality of Jenny possibly being with McNair again began to sink in, though nothing was certain. Why would she call me if he was there? The question gnawed at me. Did he leave her to deal with this on her own?

When I got home, I searched online for any mention of McNair being arrested. Nothing. But there she was—her name listed in the booking report. Anger and confusion consumed me. Why would she take the fall for him? Why didn't he handle this if he was there? I tried to make sense of it but couldn't.

I sent Jenny a text the next day:

"Jenny, I've given you every chance. I told you it was either me or him, and you've made your choice. Call him next time you need help. Your truck was impounded, and he can get it out."

I didn't expect a response, and I didn't get one.

CHAPTER 5

THE DAY BEFORE

The following day after the DUI incident brought no reply from Jenny, though I hadn't expected one. Still, the silence weighed on me. When I woke up, there was no text, no call—just the stark realization that things were unraveling faster than I could grasp. I tried to busy myself, taking care of errands and preparing for work, focusing on what I could control. But no matter how hard I tried, thoughts of Jenny and the events of the night before lingered like a storm cloud.

At work that evening, the weight of it all hung heavy. My mind wandered back to the near-reconciliation we had in Hawaii and how quickly everything fell apart after that. It felt surreal that we were now in this place, where we couldn't even have a conversation without tension. The Fourth of July loomed, and the celebratory energy around me only amplified my unease. Fireworks, laughter, and excitement from customers contrasted sharply with the turmoil inside me.

Later that night, unable to shake my frustration, I reached out to Katie, a girl I had been talking to on and off. Jenny had subtly questioned me about Katie before, though I'd always been vague in my responses. This time, I didn't hold back. If Jenny could move on, so could I—or so I told myself. I called Katie and invited her over.

Katie and I spent the evening watching a new movie that had just came out, Paranormal Activity. She seemed at ease, laughing and joking, while I tried to focus on anything but the thoughts swirling in my head. Midway through the movie, a loud, forceful knock echoed through the apartment. With the movie already being as scary as it was the knock startled both of us.

I froze for a moment, unsure of who could possibly be at my door that late at night. I glanced out of my upstairs bay window but saw nothing out of the ordinary—no unfamiliar cars, no visitors I recognized. Before I could process it, the knocking escalated into pounding, with what sounded like a shoulder slamming against the door.

"Who is it?" I yelled, my voice firm but shaky.

Silence.

Katie stood frozen at the top of the stairs, clutching a throw pillow like it was a shield. Then the door handle began rattling violently, as if someone was desperately trying to break in. My heart raced as I yelled again, this time more forcefully. "My gun is pointed right at the door, so if you come through it, you won't make it back out!"

I wasn't armed—I didn't even have a bat—but I hoped my bluff would be enough. The rattling stopped. I peeked through the blinds, but no one was there. It was as if the person had vanished into thin air. Katie and I sat up for hours trying to make sense of what had just happened. Every theory we came up with seemed more unsettling than the last. I texted everyone in my phone that night, asking if it could have been them or if they were okay. No one admitted to it.

The next morning, I woke to a slew of responses from friends and family—all confirming they hadn't been at my door. The one person I hadn't heard from yet was Jenny. Reluctantly, I texted her.

"Let me know if that was you at my door last night. Someone was banging on it like they were trying to break it down. I even saw the handle shaking. If it was you, please let me know because I'm really freaked out."

Hours passed with no reply. I drove Katie back to her place in Mount Juliet, still rattled by the night before. By the time I got to work that evening, I had almost convinced myself that it couldn't have been Jenny. Then, halfway through my shift, my phone buzzed.

It was her.

"Yeah."

That one word stopped me in my tracks. I reread my previous text to make sure I wasn't misunderstanding. She was saying yes—it had been her at my door.

"What in the world? Why were you banging on my door like that? Why didn't you just tell me it was you? Are you okay?"

Her reply came slowly. "I'm fine."

The shortness of her responses unsettled me even more. I pressed further. "Jenny, the way you were beating on my door sounded like something was wrong. You're being really short with me. What's going on? Are you okay? You need to tell me what's up."

Minutes felt like hours as I waited for her reply. Finally, it came. "I don't want to talk about it."

I stared at that message, reading it over and over. What did she mean she didn't want to talk about it? What could have driven her to show up at my door like that and then shut down completely when I asked why? I was frustrated, confused, and worried all at once. I wanted to press her for answers, but something inside me stopped. That message would turn out to be the last thing Jenny ever said to me.

Later that evening, a close friend of mine called, asking if I could pick him up after an argument with his girlfriend. He didn't have his keys and didn't want to go home, so I told him he could crash at my place. On the way back, he unloaded his pockets and revealed he had been carrying his gun. He asked if there was somewhere he could put it so I told him to put it in the top of my closet for safekeeping.

We stayed up late talking about life, trying to distract ourselves from our individual issues. As I laid in bed that night, staring at the ceiling, I couldn't shake the feeling that something was terribly wrong. The events of the past two days weighed heavily on me, but I had no idea how much worse things were about to get.

CHAPTER 6

JULY 4TH, 2009

July 4th, 2009, began like any other day for me, despite being a holiday. I had to work that evening, so my mindset was focused on staying productive. I went downstairs and noticed my friend was already gone. He had left me a text letting me know his friend had picked him up earlier, that he didn't want to disturb me, and that he had forgotten his gun in my closet. He said he'd come back later that day to grab it. I texted him back, letting him know I had to work that night, so if he didn't pick it up before then, he could come by later in the week.

I started my day like usual, making a pot of coffee and grabbing something to eat. A missed call from my friend caught my eye, and as I was about to call him back, he called again. I answered, and the urgency in his voice immediately set me on edge.

"Where are you right now?" he asked.

"I'm at home, just doing a few things before work. What's up?"

"Are you near a TV right now?"

"Yeah, I'm standing in the living room. Why?"

"Bro, turn on the TV. Steve McNair is dead."

"What?" I said, frozen in disbelief. "Are you serious?"

"Yes, dude. It's all over the news. Turn it on now."

I quickly flipped on the TV, switching to the first news station that came to mind. There it was: "Steve McNair Found Dead in Downtown Nashville." My heart sank.

"Oh my God. What happened?" I asked.

"I don't know. There's a lot of speculation. Some people are saying he might have been robbed and shot downtown. On Broadway."

"On Broadway? Seriously? That doesn't make sense. How does someone kill Steve McNair on Broadway on a weekend and get away?"

"I don't know, man. Apparently, it just happened, or they just found out. It's crazy."

We sat in stunned silence, listening to the news unfold. I was trying to process the shock of it all when my friend brought up the one person now racing through my mind.

"Have you talked to Jenny at all? I don't know where y'all stand, but maybe she knows something."

My heart stopped. Jenny. Why hadn't I thought of her? Why hadn't I heard from her?

"I haven't heard from her, man. Not in a couple of days."

"Bro, you might need to call her. Just to check and make sure she's okay."

"You're right. I'll call her now," I said, hanging up.

I dialed Jenny's number, my hands trembling. The phone rang, but it went to voicemail. I called again. Voicemail. I sent her a text:

"Hey, please call or text me back. I just saw the news. I just want to make sure you're okay."

Minutes passed with no reply. I tried to reassure myself that she was just in shock or maybe talking to the police. But the longer I waited, the more uneasy I felt. I called my oldest sister, Bootsie, for reassurance.

"Have you talked to Jenny?" she asked after I explained the situation.

"No, not a word in days," I admitted.

"Well, I'm sure she's fine, Keith. She's probably just in shock or dealing with the police. Don't let your mind go to dark places."

Her optimism helped momentarily, but the dread lingered. My other sister, Leeanne, called shortly after.

"Hey, what's going on?" she asked.

"Steve McNair is dead," I blurted out. "And I haven't heard from Jenny in 2 days."

"What?! Are you serious?? Keith, you need to go check on her," she said firmly. "If she's not answering your calls or texts, you don't really have another option."

My dad called shortly after. He, too, urged me to go check on her. "Son, if you want me to drive you, I will," he offered.

The calls kept coming. Everyone seemed to know about Jenny's connection to Steve McNair, and now they were reaching out to me for answers. The weight of it all was suffocating.

Then came a breaking news update: Steve McNair hadn't been found alone. A young woman was also found dead in the condo, but her identity had not been confirmed. My heart dropped.

I collapsed to my knees, tears streaming down my face as I begged, "Please, God. Please don't let that be Jenny. Please."

A knock at the door interrupted my anguish. It was my dad and Bootsie. They tried their best to console me, offering hugs and prayers. Shortly after, my friend arrived with a friend of his. He walked in, took a long look at me, and hugged me.

"You okay?" he asked.

"Best I can be right now," I said, tears in my eyes. "I just need to know Jenny's okay."

"I'm sure she's fine. Everything's going to be okay," he said, trying to reassure me. Then, looking toward his friend, he said, "Hey, can I grab my stuff?"

It dawned on me what he meant. "Yeah, of course," I said. He ran upstairs to grab his gun. I followed him, and as I walked into the room, I noticed him carefully counting the bullets.

"They're all there, bro," I said, almost disappointed but understanding why he was doing it.

He looked up at me, his face blank. "I know they are. I just had to make sure."

"I understand," I said quietly, the moment hanging heavy between us. It was the first time I realized someone might actually think I had something to do with what happened.

"I gotta get out of here," he said, placing the gun back in his bag. "I'll be back to check on you later tonight, okay?"

He gave me another hug before leaving.

Not long after, my sister Bootsie pointed out a Subway bag on the side table by the couch while she was picking up other things to throw away from the table. It was hidden behind a lamp, and I hadn't noticed it before. When I saw it, I froze. It was the bag from the day Jenny had come over to use the computer. The sight of it hit me like a ton of bricks.

I gripped the bag and began sobbing uncontrollably. "Please, God, let Jenny be okay. Please, I'm begging you."

My dad and sisters rushed over, holding me as I cried on the floor, clutching the bag. My dad lifted me up and hugged me tightly.

"Do you want us all to go over there? Do you want to go to her apartment and check on her? I'll drive everyone," he said.

Both of my sisters agreed. "It's the best thing to do at this point," Leeanne said. I nodded, wiping away tears, and we all loaded into my dad's truck to head to Cherry Creek Apartments.

When we got to Cherry Creek Apartments, I couldn't shake the dreadful sinking feeling in my gut that something was terribly wrong. No matter how much I tried to push it away, it only intensified. That feeling grew even worse when we pulled into the parking lot, and it started pouring rain. It reminded me of every movie or TV show where rain is used as a symbol of something tragic or heartbreaking. It rained the day my grandfather passed away too. I sat there thinking to myself, Please, God, don't let this be one of those signs.

We parked in front of Jenny's building, and my sister Leeanne turned to me. "Do you want me to go up and knock on the door?" she asked.

I felt a responsibility to be the one to go, but before I could decide, she said, "I'm just going to go up. You stay right here."

Leeanne got out and ran up to the door while Bootsie sat beside me in the backseat, trying to reassure me. "Everything's fine, Keith. Don't worry. Jenny's probably just out or not feeling up to talking. You'll see."

I wanted to believe her, but my stomach twisted tighter with each second that passed. We watched as Leeanne stood at Jenny's door, looking puzzled. I must have missed the first time she knocked because her hand suddenly went up to the door again—but this time, she gently pushed it open. My heart sank further as I saw the confusion on her face.

Leeanne turned to look back at us and then started toward the car. When she got in, her expression confirmed my fears. "Jenny's door is open, it was already open when I got up there" she said.

"What?" we all asked in unison.

"It's open. Like...cracked open. It was already open when I got up to the door," she said.

"Why would the door be open?" I asked, my voice trembling.

"I have no idea but I didn't see anyone, though. The lights were off, and it didn't seem like anyone was there." She paused, her voice lowering. "I have a bad feeling about this."

I didn't know what to say. My mind was spinning. "Did you go inside?" I asked.

"No, I didn't. I thought about it, but..." She trailed off before adding, "Should I?"

"No," everyone said almost in unison.

"But what if she's in there?" Leeanne said, her voice shaking. "What if she's hurt, or... what if she needs help?"

Before we could respond, a woman approached the car. She was middle-aged and looked concerned. "Do you know the girl who lives there?" she asked.

"Yes," Leeanne said, "we heard the news, and we came to check on her."

The woman nodded. "I haven't seen her in a couple of days, but she's always been so nice and polite. Always said hello when we crossed paths." She paused. "I've seen Steve around here a couple of times too. It's concerning I haven't seen her since the news broke."

"Do you know why her door might be open?" Leeanne asked. "Have you seen anyone coming or going from her apartment?"

The woman hesitated. "Well... earlier today, I saw a silver car parked out front. Two men—both dressed in all black—were going in and out of her apartment. They were carrying trash bags full of stuff and loading them into the trunk."

"What?" Leeanne said sharply. "That doesn't sound right."

"No, it doesn't," I added, tears welling in my eyes. My voice broke as I said, "Something is definitely wrong."

I got out of the car when I noticed my friend Antonio was standing outside. I noticed he'd walked up to the door and looked puzzled as well.

"Bro, her door is open but nobody is there." he said when I walked up.

"Yeah my sister said the same thing, how do you know nobody is there?" I replied.

"I yelled for Jenny through the door and nobody answered, it looks dark in there." he said.

My dad quickly stepped in. "Do you want to go down to the police station, son? If we go, they might be able to tell us something for sure."

I didn't feel ready to hear the truth if it was bad, but I knew he was right. I nodded. "Yes," I said softly. "That's the only way we'll know."

At the station, we all walked in together. My dad spoke on my behalf. "This is my son. His ex-girlfriend, Sahel Kazemi, is missing. We all heard the news about Steve McNair, and we know she was involved with him on and off. We're here to make sure she's okay. He's really worried, and we're all hoping for good news."

The officer listened and nodded. "Let me go check and see what I can find out," he said.

A few moments later, he returned. "Right now, we know there was another young woman at the scene. Both individuals were found deceased. But I can't share any further details about her identity at this time."

My dad pressed further. "Can you at least tell us it's not her?"

The officer shook his head. "I don't know for sure. I can't tell you anything else."

We thanked him for his time and left. The car ride back to my apartment was silent, except for the sound of the rain against the windows. My mind raced with every worst-case scenario imaginable. My tears fell silently as I prayed, Please, God. Please let her be okay.

When we got back to my apartment, the air was heavy with unspoken fears. There wasn't much conversation, and any attempt to lighten the mood felt forced. It was evident that the optimism we'd tried so hard to hold onto was fading fast. Everyone was worried, and it showed.

Here and there, someone would speak up, trying to rationalize the situation or offer words of encouragement. "Maybe it's not her. Maybe she's just staying with a friend or laying low," Bootsie said at one point. Leeanne nodded, trying to agree, but the uncertainty in her eyes betrayed her words. My dad sat quietly, occasionally glancing at me, as if to gauge whether I was holding up.

I tried to listen to their reassurances, but with every minute that passed, it felt harder and harder to believe. The new details being reported on the news were becoming increasingly difficult to ignore. The pieces weren't adding up in any way that could bring comfort.

Then it happened.

The news anchor broke in with the update that shattered everything: the identity of the young woman found with Steve McNair had been confirmed. My heart dropped into my stomach. It was Sahel Kazemi.

It was Jenny.

It's a moment I'll never forget. A moment that will haunt me for the rest of my life. A moment that changed everything. Forever.

The confirmation came later in the day, and it was like the world just stopped. I remember seeing it—the news finally released the name of the woman who was found dead with Steve McNair: Sahel Kazemi. Jenny. My Jenny. Everything inside me shattered at that moment. It felt like the air was ripped out of my lungs, and I couldn't breathe. I don't even remember what I was doing when I heard it, but I know that when her name came across the screen, my entire world collapsed.

The whole day, I'd been trying to shake this unshakable feeling that something was wrong. I kept telling myself it was just my mind playing tricks on me, that I was overthinking, that I'd hear from Jenny eventually. Even after going to her apartment and finding the door open, I still held on to some shred of hope that there was a logical explanation. Maybe she was with a friend. Maybe she just needed time. Anything to avoid facing what I was terrified might be true.

But when her name came out on the news, all of that hope disappeared. The truth hit me like a freight train—Jenny was gone.

I can't even put into words the flood of emotions that followed. First, there was shock. A numbness that made everything around me feel distant and surreal, like I was watching my own life happen to someone else. Then, grief—an all-consuming sorrow that crushed me under its weight. And beneath it all, there was anger. Not just anger at what had happened, but anger at how quickly the media began to twist the narrative.

"Murder-suicide." Those words rang out like a punch to the gut. They were everywhere. Reporters, commentators, even people online—all jumping to the same conclusion, painting Jenny as a jealous, angry woman who had done the unthinkable. The Jenny they described wasn't the Jenny I knew. She was kind, thoughtful, full of life and laughter. She loved deeply and fiercely, and she wouldn't have hurt anyone, especially not like that.

Hearing them reduce her to nothing more than a headline broke me in ways I didn't know were possible. I was already struggling to process her death, and now I had to watch the world drag her name through the mud, turning her into someone I knew she wasn't. It was infuriating. It was wrong. And it left me with a feeling I still carry to this day—a need to set the record straight.

In that moment, though, I couldn't focus on any of that. All I could feel was the unbearable weight of losing her. The grief, the questions, the confusion—it all came crashing down on me at once, and for the first time, I realized just how much this would change my life forever. The person I had loved so deeply, the person who had been such a huge part of my world, was gone. And there was nothing I could do to bring her back.

After the confirmation of Jenny's passing, everything around me felt like it came to a standstill. The world that had already felt heavy now seemed unbearable. I couldn't process it—how someone I had loved so deeply, someone I still cared for, was gone. My mind spiraled as memories of our time together collided with the harsh reality that I would never see her again. I felt paralyzed, as though time itself had stopped.

The first conversations I had after the news broke were with my family. My dad and sisters were still there, and their presence was the only thing keeping me from completely breaking down. But even they were at a loss. Their voices wavered between shock and sorrow as they struggled to find the right words, though there were none. "Are you okay?" "Do you need anything?" they asked over and over, but I could only shake my head, unable to speak. I was too overwhelmed to even begin to answer.

Friends started reaching out too, their messages and calls flooding my phone. Their condolences were heartfelt, but the disbelief in their voices mirrored my own. Some asked, "Do you think she really did it?" Hearing those words wasn't easy. It hurt deeply to hear people even consider that possibility. But at the same time, I understood. Given the circumstances and the narrative already being pushed by the media, I couldn't blame anyone for having questions. Still, it was a painful reminder of how little control I had over how Jenny was being portrayed. It broke my heart because I knew the person she was, and I knew in my soul that she wasn't capable of what they were accusing her of.

Emotionally, I was torn apart. The grief was unbearable, but it was mixed with this boiling frustration. The media had barely begun covering the story, and yet they were already twisting her memory, painting her as something she wasn't. They didn't know Jenny like I did. They didn't see the kindness, the love, the joy she brought to the people in her life. All they saw was a scandal, and they were quick to exploit it.

The rest of the day passed in a blur. I didn't eat. I didn't sleep. I couldn't even move from the spot where I had heard her name on the news. My mind replayed everything from the past few days—the unease when I first heard about Steve McNair, the black SUV outside the condo, going to Jenny's apartment and finding her door cracked open. The signs were there, but I had refused to believe them. Now, I couldn't deny what had happened, no matter how much I wanted to.

One moment that stands out vividly was sitting alone, staring at my phone. The calls and texts kept coming—friends, family, even people I hadn't spoken to in years—but I couldn't bring myself to respond to most of them. Their words, their pity, their questions—it was all too much.

After everyone had gone home, Leeanne called and I just broke down immediately. I cried harder than I ever had before, and she stayed on the line with me, listening as I poured out everything I was feeling.

Later that night, I made the mistake of turning on the news again. The coverage was relentless. Reporters were outside Steve McNair's condo, outside Jenny's family's home. They dissected every detail of her life, twisting it to fit their narrative. They were calling her a "jealous mistress," a "murderer." Seeing her face on the screen, paired with those words, made me physically ill. That wasn't the Jenny I knew. I wanted to scream, to tell them they were wrong, but I couldn't. I felt powerless.

That day didn't just break me—it changed me. The grief, the pain, the unanswered questions—they would shape everything that came next. It wasn't just about losing Jenny. It was about losing her to a story that I knew wasn't true, to a world that would never fully understand who she was. And even now, the weight of that day remains, a constant reminder of everything I lost.

The immediate public and media response to the tragedy surrounding Steve McNair and Jenny's deaths was overwhelming, and it impacted me in ways I still struggle to fully articulate. The media frenzy began almost immediately after the news broke, and within hours, they had already constructed a narrative—a narrative that was as devastating as it was unfair.

They labeled it a murder-suicide before any official ruling was ever made, claiming that Jenny, consumed by jealousy or emotional instability, had likely killed Steve and then herself. This narrative was everywhere—on TV, in newspapers, and online—and it spread like wildfire. Seeing her face on the screen, paired with words like "jealous girlfriend" and "murderer," was gut-wrenching. The media didn't know her. They didn't know the kind, loving, and hopeful person she was. They didn't care about the truth—they cared about a sensational story, and Jenny was their scapegoat.

Personally, this narrative was unbearable. I had already lost someone I cared deeply for, and now I was forced to watch as her memory was twisted into something unrecognizable. It felt like they were robbing her of her humanity, reducing her to a caricature of a "scorned woman" for the sake of headlines. It wasn't just hurtful—it was infuriating.

I knew in my heart that Jenny wasn't capable of what they were accusing her of, but I felt powerless to change the story being told.

The public response compounded the pain. People I knew, and even strangers, began asking me questions—some out of concern, others out of morbid curiosity. "Do you think she really did it?" "Did you see this coming?" These questions were like daggers. They assumed the media's version of events was true and expected me to provide answers I didn't have. It felt like the world was piling on, and I was stuck in the middle of a storm I didn't ask for.

Emotionally, I was drowning. The grief of losing Jenny was already more than I could bear, but the added weight of the media and public judgment made it feel like I couldn't breathe. I felt isolated, even with family and friends around me, because no one could truly understand what I was going through. The person I had loved was gone, and now her memory was being tarnished in ways that felt deeply unfair and untrue.

Coping during those early days was incredibly difficult. I didn't eat. I didn't sleep. My mind was consumed by questions: How did this happen? Why did this happen? I replayed the events of that day over and over in my head, trying to make sense of it all, but there were no answers—only more pain. I avoided most phone calls and texts because I couldn't deal with the pity, the speculation, or the questions. The only people I allowed close were my sisters, my dad and a few others who understood that sometimes, I just needed silence.

One of the ways I coped, though not necessarily in a healthy way, was by fixating on the inconsistencies in the media's narrative. I couldn't accept the story they were telling because it didn't align with the Jenny I knew. She wasn't angry or unstable. She was kind, loving, and full of life. These thoughts consumed me, and I found myself diving deeper into the details of the case, looking for anything that might explain the truth. It was a way of holding onto her memory, of defending who she truly was, even when the world seemed determined to tear her down.

Ultimately, the media and public response left scars that I still carry. It wasn't just about losing Jenny—it was about losing her in such a public and brutal way, with her name dragged through the mud by people who didn't know her. It shaped how I view the world and the way people consume tragedies.

To this day, I still fight to tell the truth about Jenny, not just for her memory, but for myself and everyone who truly knew her. That fight has become part of my healing, even though I've accepted the pain will always be there.

CHAPTER 7

EYE OF THE STORM

I had no idea of the magnitude of what was to come. Just trying to wrap my head around the fact that Jenny was gone was enough to paralyze me. But what happened next? I was nowhere near prepared for it.

In the immediate days following her death, I started noticing my name mentioned in local media reports. At first, it was subtle—a passing mention of our connection—but it didn't take long before my name became a focal point. The more it was mentioned, the more people online and on social media began to speculate. The armchair detectives emerged, piecing together their theories, and before I knew it, I was being pinned as the person responsible for their deaths.

The local media began labeling me a "person of interest." They dug into my past, pulling out anything they could spin into a salacious story. They discovered my music, dissecting every lyric as though it held some hidden confession. My songs, written months and even years earlier, were about my experiences growing up in Antioch—a tough environment where drugs, violence, and hardship were part of daily life. Music had been my outlet, a way to express and process my reality. But to the media, those lyrics became evidence of a dark, violent persona. They completely ignored the timestamps and context of the songs, twisting them into something they were never meant to be.

The more the media fueled their narrative, the more the public turned on me. Social media became a war zone. For every message of condolence, there were dozens of hate-filled comments and death threats. Strangers sent me messages accusing me of being a monster, while others threatened to take justice into their own hands. The media frenzy spilled into my real life, too. Reporters started showing up at my job, my apartment, my dad's house, and even my sisters' homes. They tracked down family members, asking invasive questions they couldn't possibly answer. It became clear that they weren't searching for the truth—they were chasing a headline, no matter the cost.

I contacted the police about the death threats. I showed them the messages flooding my inbox, reading aloud the vile things people were saying. Their response was infuriatingly dismissive: "Unless something happens, there's nothing we can do. Save the messages, and let us know if anything happens." That was it. My life was being threatened, my name was being dragged through the mud, and the police couldn't—or wouldn't—help.

Feeling helpless, I deleted all my social media accounts. I hoped it would bring me some peace, but it only made things worse. To the public, my disappearance from social media looked like an admission of guilt, like I was running away instead of trying to protect myself. The speculation only grew louder, and the attacks more vicious.

Even my friends weren't spared. Matt, who had been nothing but supportive, got pulled into the narrative because of a Facebook post he had written days before Jenny's death. In the post, he vented his frustration in response to Steve McNair letting Jenny take the fall for the DUI. Unfortunately, the post didn't display the correct timestamp, making it seem like he had written it after their deaths. The media seized on this, suggesting that my friend was somehow involved, and dragged his name through the mud too.

He did everything right. He went to the police, explained the situation, and provided proof that the post was made before their deaths. The police cleared him, but by then, the damage was done. The public had already made up their minds, and no amount of truth could undo the harm caused by the media's narrative.

I tried to keep going, but it was impossible. The reporters wouldn't leave me alone. They swarmed my workplace, forcing me to take time off. White Castle granted me two weeks, but even that didn't feel like enough. My sister Leeanne invited me to stay with her in Lebanon to get away from the chaos, and I took her up on the offer. For a few days, it was a much-needed reprieve, but somehow, the media found me there too. They started knocking on her door, relentless in their pursuit of a statement.

One day, I walked to a nearby gas station, trying to keep a low profile with my hood up. As I approached, I heard someone shout my name. Instinctively, I turned to look, only to see a car abruptly U-turn and speed toward me. A man leaned out the window, yelling something threatening. My heart raced as I quickened my pace, heading straight for the gas station. The car pulled into the parking lot, and two men got out, their expressions making it clear they didn't have good intentions.

By some miracle, as I reached the gas station door, a police officer walked out. The two men froze, turned around, and got back in their car. I'll never forget the way they looked at me—or the relief I felt when they drove away. I didn't know who they were, but the fact that they were willing to confront me, possibly harm me, over something I had nothing to do with was terrifying.

Back at Leeanne's house, I sat in silence, trying to make sense of everything. The media had turned my life upside down. They had vilified me, painted me as a killer, and left me with no way to defend myself. I hovered over the delete button on my music page, my heart heavy with the realization of what I was about to do. Music had been my outlet, my passion, my escape. But now, it was being used against me. With a deep breath, I clicked delete, watching years of work disappear in an instant.

Even with all the precautions I took, the world wouldn't let me move on. Everywhere I went, there were whispers, stares, and threats. I was trapped, powerless against the storm the media had created, and I had no idea how to make it stop.

The way the media handled my music during the aftermath of Jenny and Steve McNair's deaths was disheartening on a level I can't fully describe. Music had always been my outlet, a way to process emotions and experiences from growing up in Antioch. Like any artist, I wanted my music to be heard, to make an impact, but not like this. The exposure I got wasn't the kind that anyone would want—it was toxic and twisted beyond recognition.

One song in particular, Closed Casket, became their focal point. That song came from a deeply personal and painful situation involving my family. It was born out of frustration, betrayal, and a need to express the anger I felt at that time. I used an instrumental from one of Eminem's tracks, also titled Closed Casket, and wrote my own version, venting about the pain caused by someone who had hurt people I loved. It was meant to stay private, something I only intended to share with a few trusted friends. But it leaked. Once the damage was done, I decided to just release it publicly, never imagining it would one day be weaponized against me.

The lyrics of Closed Casket were raw, emotional, and angry—admittedly, they didn't paint a pretty picture. I was venting my emotions, not making threats I intended to act on, but the media didn't care about context. They fixated on lines about betrayal and violence, twisting them to fit their narrative. They argued that the song wasn't about a personal family matter at all but a premeditated confession about Jenny and McNair. The fact that the song had been written and published months before their deaths—clearly dated—didn't matter to them. They ignored those facts entirely.

Hearing the media twist my lyrics to fit their agenda was devastating. They made me out to be a violent, unhinged person, capitalizing on stereotypes about the kind of people who came out of Antioch. Worse, the silence from the police only fueled the speculation. I was in constant contact with law enforcement, providing everything I could to help them, but they weren't saying anything publicly to clear my name. Instead, the media ran wild, painting me as a killer, a jealous ex, and even as someone who might have orchestrated a murder-suicide.

One of the most difficult moments came when CBS Investigates reached out. They presented themselves as professional and fair, promising to let me tell my side of the story. They assured me I could speak openly, defend myself, and defend Jenny. That was all I wanted—to set the record straight, to make it clear that I was innocent and that Jenny wasn't the person they were portraying her to be.

The interview was recorded downtown, lasting over three hours. I opened up about everything—the days leading up to their deaths, the men seen leaving Jenny's apartment with trash bags, and my belief that neither Jenny nor I had anything to do with this. But the promises they made before the interview were quickly broken. Toward the end, they blindsided me with questions they had sworn not to ask. I did my best to stay composed, but I felt betrayed. When the interview aired, my three hours of testimony were reduced to ten minutes of carefully edited soundbites. They cherry-picked the moments that fit their narrative, leaving out everything I'd said to defend myself and Jenny. That experience solidified my decision never to speak to the media again.

Finally, after weeks of silence, the Nashville police chief publicly stated that I was no longer a suspect. But even then, they didn't explain why I had been investigated in the first place or what evidence had cleared me. The truth was simple: they had security footage proving I was at work the entire night, making it impossible for me to have been involved. They had that footage within days of the tragedy but chose to stay silent, leaving me to face the fallout alone.

Their lack of action allowed the media's narrative to solidify, and no press conference could undo the damage.

The aftermath of that silence and misrepresentation still lingers. To this day, there are people who believe I was involved, people who refuse to let go of the false narrative spun by the media. And in my opinion, the Nashville Police Department bears much of the blame. They had the truth all along but withheld it, allowing the media to fill the void with lies. It wasn't just my name they tarnished—it was Jenny's as well. And for that, I'll never forgive them.

The media attention, public scrutiny, and accusations profoundly impacted my relationships with family and friends. It also forced me to search within myself, digging deeper than I ever had before, to rediscover a sense of self amidst the chaos. Losing Jenny left me shattered in a way I could never have anticipated. When I say the grief made me wish I had died alongside her, I mean it in the most literal sense. The pain was unbearable, and the additional pressure from external forces only magnified it.

In the weeks following the tragedy, the cracks in relationships began to show. Everyone around me had their own theories and beliefs about what had happened, and those beliefs often clashed. My stance was clear: I never believed Jenny did what they were saying. I was open about this with anyone who would listen, but not everyone agreed. Family and friends started to form their own ideas based on the media narrative and the police's declarations. This created an uncomfortable tension, even among those closest to me.

Over time, a divide emerged. I naturally gravitated toward the people who shared my belief in Jenny's innocence. These were the individuals who supported me, who listened, and who truly understood my pain. On the other side were those who either believed the official story or were unsure, and while some tried to hide it, their hesitation was palpable. Conversations became strained, and the weight of unspoken judgments lingered in the air. It was exhausting.

The media's persistence didn't help. Reporters were still reaching out to family and friends, and some participated in interviews that left me feeling betrayed. Comments made in those interviews, whether intentional or not, added fuel to the fire. Hearing those things hurt deeply, and it made me instinctively distance myself from certain people. I had to protect my mental health, and that meant stepping away from anyone who wasn't contributing to my healing.

There were pivotal moments during this time- discussions, disagreements, even arguments- that defined how I moved forward. Some relationships ended permanently because of what was said or how I felt people had handled the situation. It was heartbreaking, but it was also necessary. Those moments forced me to reassess who I allowed in my life and to focus on surrounding myself with positivity and understanding.

Looking back, this period was a turning point. While the divide was painful, it ultimately clarified who I could count on and who I couldn't. It taught me the importance of prioritizing my own well-being and surrounding myself with people who truly cared for me and supported me through the darkest time of my life. It was a life-defining chapter, and while it was filled with heartbreak, it also set the foundation for the strength I needed to keep moving forward.

It really started to hit me that my life would probably never be the same when I tried getting back onto social media again. Things had finally started to die down as far as local media coverage went—they weren't hounding my job or my apartment anymore. But little did I know that the chaos they caused had been acting as a distraction from the immense pain and depression festering inside me.

The drastic increase in smoking, the lack of eating, and the sleepless nights were taking a major toll on my body. While I had been surrounded by both negative public attention and positive encouragement from family and friends, I hadn't realized how much their presence, however overwhelming, had kept me from spiraling further. When the media moved on to other stories and the phone calls from family turned into occasional check-ins, I was left with just myself—and all the broken pieces around me.

Jenny was gone. Steve McNair was gone. The world had pinned it on her, and so many believed I had to have been involved. The silence in my apartment was unbearable. For the first time in my life, I felt a pain that I couldn't even begin to describe. Falling asleep became impossible, and waking up when I did manage to sleep felt like a chore. During the day, I moved on autopilot. Returning to work offered no solace. People I was close to were supportive, but I could feel the stares and whispers from others who clearly had their doubts. I didn't want to be at work, but I didn't want to be anywhere. I wished I didn't exist.

My job performance plummeted. They moved me around, hoping it would shake things up and help, but nothing worked. Life at home was even worse. I spent hours obsessing over the details surrounding the case, chain-smoking cigarettes while lost in thought, or crying silently in some corner of my apartment. At times, I lashed out, overwhelmed by everything I was carrying inside. I knew I couldn't continue this way—I had to do something, or I was going to self-destruct.

I decided to test the waters and see if I could re-enter social media. I created a Facebook account and gave it some time before I started posting. At first, it felt nice. The interactions brought some noise back into the silence of my life, and I found comfort in sharing my thoughts. Without music as my outlet, I started writing notes about how I was feeling. For a short time, the feedback from others felt uplifting.

But that relief didn't last long. Before I knew it, the hate mail and vile messages started pouring in. It became impossible to block out the negativity. I realized it was too soon, and I wondered if I'd ever be able to escape the online torment. I deleted my account again, and the silence returned—only this time, it felt heavier. Conversations over the phone or through text didn't help. They always led back to the tragedy, and instead of comfort, they only seemed to amplify my pain.

Desperate for relief, I decided to try something I'd never done before: therapy. I spoke to people at work who helped me set up my first sessions with a therapist. At first, I felt hopeful. Those initial visits gave me a safe space to unload everything I had been keeping inside. It felt good knowing I could finally share my thoughts with someone who was truly listening—and being paid to do so.

We started with my childhood and worked our way through my young adult years. I deliberately refrained from telling the therapist why I was really there at first because I didn't want my grief to overshadow everything else. But once the topic of Jenny's death and the case came to light, everything changed.

I saw the way my therapist began looking at me differently. The questions became sharper, more probing, as though they were searching for something incriminating. It became painfully clear that they weren't just there to help—they were curious, almost fascinated by the case itself. I felt like I was being interrogated rather than supported. That realization broke me. It made me feel like I couldn't trust anyone, not even someone who was supposed to help me heal.

The other side of therapy that turned me away was the medication they prescribed almost immediately. The sleep medication they gave me didn't help me sleep—it caused hallucinations and horrific dreams. On top of that, the medication for anxiety and depression didn't alleviate my symptoms but worsened them. My depression deepened, and I started having suicidal thoughts—something I had never experienced before. It felt like the treatment was more experimental than intentional, as though I was a case study rather than a person who desperately needed help.

This combination of experiences changed my view of therapy and medication for mental health for years to come. I left therapy that day and never went back—not for over a decade. That experience solidified my negative perception of therapy, and it would take years for me to even consider seeking help again.

As time passed, discussions and rumors about the case were everywhere—on social media, in the news, and in conversations I couldn't avoid. The official proclamation by the Metropolitan Police Department deemed the tragedy a murder-suicide, blaming Jenny entirely. They cited gunpowder residue on her hand and claimed the weapon was found beneath her body. But the more I researched, the more questions arose.

Details from the autopsy alone left me baffled. The gunpowder residue was found on Jenny's non-dominant hand, opposite the side of her head where the entry wound was located. How could someone with no history of handling firearms shoot herself in such a manner? The idea of her awkwardly reaching across her face to pull the trigger defied logic. It felt like the official story was asking the world to believe something that simply didn't make sense.

Adding to this, I knew Jenny better than anyone. I had spent four years with her, seen her best and worst moments, and never once did I feel unsafe around her. She couldn't even kill a spider in our apartment—how could she have committed such a brutal act? It wasn't just painful to consider; it was impossible to believe.

Jenny's family shared similar doubts, and I found solace in their interviews, where they, too, voiced their disbelief. Others began speaking out as well, questioning the case's inconsistencies and even defending Jenny. It felt like a small glimmer of hope in a sea of accusations. But the most significant breakthrough came when a former police officer and private investigator, Vincent Hill, reached out to me.

Vincent believed in Jenny's innocence as strongly as I did. He reached out online, saying he had uncovered evidence that could reopen the case, and asked to meet with me. When we met, he laid out everything he had found, filling in gaps I hadn't even considered. He asked me questions about my relationship with Jenny and the events leading up to her death, and I gave him everything I could. His determination was inspiring. He planned to write a book exposing the truth and use it to push for a reinvestigation.

Sadly, despite his efforts, the Metropolitan Police Department refused to reopen the case. His book was published, exposing glaring inconsistencies, but much of the public dismissed it as a conspiracy theory. It was heartbreaking to see his work and Jenny's truth brushed aside by a world that had already made up its mind.

Meanwhile, details about McNair's personal life began to emerge. He was no longer just Nashville's beloved "Golden Boy"; he was now a known womanizer. Stories came out about how he charmed young women, spinning tales of impending divorce and false promises of marriage. Jenny had believed those promises. According to her, he even met her family and assured them he was in love with her and would marry her. I began to understand how she had fallen for him, but I couldn't reconcile the idea of her becoming a "scorned woman" capable of murder. That wasn't the Jenny I knew.

If anyone had reason to feel scorned, wouldn't it have been McNair's wife? Where was she in all of this? These thoughts swirled in my mind as I continued to uncover more details. Rumors and speculation fueled by the media only added to the chaos, but nothing could prepare me for the explosive revelations still to come. These weren't just inconsistencies—they were glaring holes in the official narrative, pouring gasoline on the fire of my belief in Jenny's innocence.

As time passed, the discussions and rumors surrounding the case were relentless. The proclamation by the Metropolitan Police Department declaring the case a murder-suicide weighed heavily on my mind, especially as I continued to find inconsistencies in the official narrative. But it wasn't just the case itself that consumed me; it was the reaction of the public and my own growing determination to speak out, despite the risks.

The fire inside me to defend Jenny's name and prove her innocence was fueled by both the questionable details surrounding the case and the way the world had so quickly vilified her. I tried to rationalize what had happened and how to move forward, but the weight of it all was suffocating. I knew I needed to speak up, but I was torn. Speaking out could stir the pot and potentially put not just me, but my loved ones, in danger. The possibility that the person responsible for Jenny and McNair's deaths was still out there was terrifying. What if they came after me next?

These thoughts brought back memories of the night someone had been pounding on my door, the fear I felt, and the police's response when I asked if it had been Jenny. They told me they couldn't confirm anything, and that uncertainty had haunted me ever since. What if that wasn't Jenny at my door that night? What if Jenny was already gone, and someone else was using her phone to cover their tracks? These questions swirled in my mind, and the fear of speaking out paralyzed me for a long time.

But the fear couldn't hold me forever. Eventually, I decided I had to act. I had to speak up, not just for Jenny, but for myself. I poured my thoughts and knowledge into a song I titled "My Opinion." It was raw, emotional, and unapologetic. I detailed every inconsistency I had uncovered and every belief I held about the case. It wasn't just a song—it was my truth.

When I finished recording and uploading the track, I hovered over the "Post" button for what felt like an eternity. My heart raced as I thought about what I was about to do. Then, I closed my eyes and clicked the button. The song was live on SoundClick, ReverbNation, and my recreated MySpace music page. I knew this was a risk, but I was determined to let the world hear my voice. If people were going to talk about me, they could at least hear my words directly.

The song began gaining traction, and comments started pouring in. Many people shared my sentiment, expressing support and belief in Jenny's innocence. Others, of course, left hateful messages, further pushing the narrative that had been cemented in the public's mind. But for the first time in months, I felt a spark of purpose. I blocked out the negativity and focused on the people who believed in the truth I was trying to share.

However, that sense of purpose didn't last long. Late one night, I was outside on my porch smoking a cigarette when I noticed a black SUV parked on the side street near my apartment. The side street wasn't used often, and there was no logical reason for anyone to be parked there. I shrugged it off as a coincidence, but the next night, the SUV was there again—this time with its headlights on.

By the third night, I was on edge. The same SUV, in the same spot, with its headlights beaming toward my apartment. Something wasn't right. My frustration boiled over, and I flicked my cigarette in the direction of the SUV before walking toward it, arms gesturing angrily.

"Are you here for me?" I yelled. "Why are you camping outside my house? Are you coming to kill me too?"

I don't know what I expected, but I needed answers. The SUV's headlights stayed on, but the vehicle didn't move. My heart pounded as I got closer, the fear and anger mixing into a dangerous cocktail of emotions. Just as I was about to reach the SUV, the engine revved, and they abruptly sped off, heading down Old Hickory Boulevard toward the interstate.

I never saw that black SUV again.

That moment solidified two things for me: speaking out was dangerous, but it was also necessary. I couldn't let fear stop me from fighting for the truth. If anything, the encounter only strengthened my resolve to push forward, no matter the risks.

The aftermath of posting "My Opinion" was a mix of emotions—both positive and negative. On one hand, it felt empowering to finally speak my truth, to express everything I had been holding in and lay it all out for the world to see. The comments from people who shared my beliefs about Jenny's innocence were encouraging, and for a brief moment, I felt like I was finally being heard. On the other hand, the unease was undeniable. The black SUV incident weighed heavily on my mind, and the strong possibility that the real killer was still out there filled me with a level of worry I hadn't experienced before.

I couldn't shake the thought that by speaking out so boldly, I might have put myself and the people I cared about in danger. Conversations with my family and close friends only reinforced those fears. They understood why I had posted the song, but they also shared my concerns about the potential consequences. I realized that as much as I wanted to defend Jenny and shine a light on the truth, I needed to be smart about how I approached it.

Reluctantly, I made the decision to remove "My Opinion" from my music pages. It wasn't an easy choice—it felt like I was silencing myself all over again. But at the time, it felt like the safest and most logical thing to do. I left the other songs up, ones that painted a picture of who Jenny really was and the love we had shared, but the risk of keeping "My Opinion" online outweighed the reward. I knew that if the killer truly was still out there, my song had put me in their sights, and I couldn't afford to take that chance.

Despite removing the song, I didn't give up on my mission to prove Jenny's innocence. I simply shifted my focus. I continued researching the case and piecing together evidence, but I did it quietly, keeping most of my findings to myself. I limited conversations about the case with family and friends, not wanting to put them in harm's way or stir up unnecessary tension. Instead, I poured my energy into bettering myself—emotionally, mentally, and physically. I refused to let the case consume me entirely, but I also refused to let it go. I just knew I had to find a healthier, more calculated way to keep fighting for Jenny without putting everything and everyone around me at risk.

CHAPTER 8

QUESTIONING THE INVESTIGATION

From the very beginning, I felt like the investigation into Jenny and Steve's deaths was rushed. It seemed like the police were eager to tie everything up in a neat bow and call it what it looked like on the surface—a murder-suicide. But as more details emerged and after talking with Vincent Hill and reading about his findings in his book over time, it became clear that there were far too many inconsistencies and unanswered questions, many of which the police completely ignored or dismissed.

The foundation of their conclusion relied on two pieces of evidence: minor traces of gunpowder residue on Jenny's left hand and the murder weapon found underneath her body. But these facts, when examined closely, didn't hold up. Jenny was right-handed, so why was the residue found on her non-dominant hand? And even more perplexing, the fatal entry wound on her head was on the right side. For someone to hold the gun in their left hand, reach across their face, and pull the trigger defies logic. Additionally, the amount of gunpowder residue was inconsistent with someone firing a gun multiple times from close range. If Jenny had fired that gun as many times as they claimed, there should have been far more residue on her skin and clothing.

The positions of the bodies also raised serious questions. Steve was slumped on the couch with two gunshots to the head and two to the chest, while Jenny was found on the floor with the gun beneath her. The trajectory of the shots and the gun's position didn't add up. How could someone fire multiple rounds, fall to the ground, and have the weapon end up neatly underneath their body? These details begged for further investigation, yet the police seemed content with their narrative.

The more I thought about it, the more it seemed like the investigation was hasty and incomplete. Why would they rush through something so significant? To me, there are only two explanations: either they wanted to avoid the negative publicity that a prolonged investigation would bring to Nashville, or there was foul play involved—something much deeper and darker.

Steve McNair was a beloved public figure and a star athlete, and I've followed football long enough to understand how much money and influence are involved, especially with someone of his stature. The idea of corruption or a deliberate cover-up wasn't far-fetched to me. Growing up in Antioch, I wasn't naïve to the possibility of police corruption. Stories of law enforcement being complicit in cover-ups for far less money and influence than what was at stake here weren't uncommon.

My doubts weren't just based on the evidence; they were also rooted in how the police handled me. When I was brought in for questioning, I was fully compliant and transparent. I answered every question and even shared information that I thought was crucial to understanding what may have happened. One of the key pieces of evidence I provided was a series of text messages where I urged Jenny not to contact Steve's wife. I believed this information could shed light on Jenny's mindset and the dynamics between her, Steve, and his wife. But despite its significance, the police seemed uninterested.

I also told them about the incident of someone banging on my door late at night, which remains one of the most chilling experiences of my life. Jenny's last text to me claimed it was her, but it didn't feel right. The person at my door sounded like a large, strong man trying to force his way in. If the police had taken the time to investigate—perhaps by pinging cell phone locations—they might have uncovered something critical. But they didn't. They dismissed it, leaving me with more questions than answers.

The actions of others involved in the case also raised red flags. Wayne Neely, the first person to discover the bodies, didn't immediately call 911. Instead, he contacted Robert Gaddy, who then waited hours before notifying the authorities. Why the delay? What were they discussing during that time? And why did Gaddy insist on being the one to call the police? It felt like they were trying to control the narrative from the very start.

Gaddy's actions following the discovery only added to my suspicions. He immediately took control of Steve's condo and other affairs, which struck me as odd. Adding to this, Gaddy and Steve's wife reportedly attended the same church, suggesting a potential connection that was never explored.

Then there was Adrian Gilliam, the man who sold Jenny the gun. Initially, he claimed he didn't know her, but phone records revealed hundreds of text messages between them, including a spike in communication the night before the tragedy. Gilliam was one of the last people to text Jenny, yet he lied about their relationship. Why? And why wasn't this explored further?

The more I pieced together these details, the less sense the official story made. It wasn't just about proving Jenny's innocence anymore—it was about uncovering the truth in a case that had been mishandled, rushed, and, in my opinion, deliberately obscured.

As I delved deeper, two questions haunted me: Who was at my door that night, and why? And did Jenny tell Steve's wife? These questions, paired with the black SUV parked near my apartment for three nights in a row, added layers of suspicion that couldn't be ignored. Was someone watching me? Was someone ensuring I wouldn't get involved?

The silence surrounding Steve's wife also raised serious questions. She never spoke publicly about the case, and the police never elaborated on her role in the investigation. Learning that she went to court to block Steve's two sons from accessing his inheritance and forced his mother out of the home he had built for her only deepened my suspicions. With no will in place, the financial motives seemed glaring.

After connecting with Vincent Hill and learning the details of his thorough investigation, my suspicions grew significantly. Vincent's findings pointed to even more troubling possibilities, including potential corruption within the Metropolitan Police Department. If someone was willing to kill to keep the truth hidden, what would stop them from coming after me or those I cared about?

Ultimately, I decided to take a step back—not because I wanted to, but because I had to. The risks outweighed the rewards, and I knew I couldn't help Jenny if I wasn't around to fight for her. Stepping back wasn't giving up; it was regrouping. I hadn't reached the end of this journey. In fact, it felt like I had only scratched the surface.

As I closed this chapter of my life, I realized that stepping back wasn't just about self-preservation—it was about finding the strength to move forward in a way that would allow me to uncover the truth without losing myself in the process.

CHAPTER 9

PICKING UP THE PIECES

When I made the decision to step back from digging into the investigation and to leave things alone, I thought it would bring me some peace. Instead, it took a heavy toll on my mental health. The depression and grief that I had worked so hard to distract myself from by focusing on proving Jenny's innocence came rushing back with full force. It was like all the emotions I had suppressed were waiting for the moment I slowed down, and they hit me like a tidal wave.

Trying to fall back into my regular life felt impossible. Everything seemed so out of place, so open-ended and unresolved. Before Jenny passed, I had a better sense of self and direction for my life, even after our breakup. The thought of possibly getting back together had always lingered in the back of my mind. But with her gone, the harsh finality of her absence slammed the door shut on that possibility. It forced me to think about and move toward a future I wasn't prepared for.

Grief is the most difficult process a person can endure. There's no instruction manual, no one-size-fits-all advice to help you navigate it. It's something you have to face on your own, in your own way. During this time, my oldest sister, Bootsie, became an anchor for me. A devout Christian with a faith stronger than anyone I've ever known, she was there for me every step of the way. I called her endlessly, pouring out my thoughts and emotions. No matter how heavy the conversation, she never failed to listen and offer her support.

Bootsie encouraged me to lean on God during this time. I hadn't picked up a Bible in years, but at her suggestion, I started again. I searched for passages that addressed grief, loss, and strength. The words brought me comfort and helped me feel less alone in my pain. I began to attend church regularly again, finding solace in the community and the act of worship.

These steps didn't fix everything, but they helped me start to move forward. Slowly but surely, I began to feel a sense of comfort and purpose returning. I found myself doing small things around the house—cleaning, rearranging furniture, even exercising a bit more. I cut back on smoking, too, though I still relied on it to get through some of the tougher moments.

The grief didn't go away entirely with time as I anticipated. There were still days and nights when I would drift into thoughts of Jenny—of what was and what could have been if things had been different. Some of those moments broke me, leaving me in tears. Other times, I found the strength to push through. It was a process, and even though I didn't know it at the time, it's one that I'm still working through to this day.

A little over six months after Jenny's passing, I found myself in a quiet moment of reflection. It was late at night, and I was lying on the couch in my loft apartment after work. The silence was heavy—no TV, no music, just the faint hum of the refrigerator. I wasn't doing much of anything, just lost in thought, trying to make sense of everything that had happened. The loneliness and the finality of Jenny's absence loomed large, and though I had been working hard to regain some semblance of normalcy, it still felt like I was swimming against the current.

I had started sorting through my phone that night, deleting old files and pictures, anything that wasn't necessary anymore. It was part of my effort to clear space, both literally and figuratively. That's when I came across the Yahoo Messenger app, something I hadn't thought about in a long time. I had created it as a way to communicate with my sister's friend during a time when my relationship with Jenny was strained. Seeing it again brought back a wave of emotions—guilt, regret, and curiosity. I knew I needed to delete the account, but when I logged in, I was stunned to see her online at that exact moment.

We had created those accounts for each other, and I hadn't spoken to her since the day I emailed her to break things off completely. I froze, unsure of what to do. The coincidence was uncanny, and it lingered in my mind as I got up to shower and prepare for bed. Should I reach out? What would I even say? I debated with myself for what felt like hours before finally typing out a simple message:

"Hey, I know it's been a while. I just wanted to see how you were. Hope everything is okay and you're doing well. Hit me up sometime if you'd like to talk."

I sent it just before going to bed, figuring nothing would come of it. The next morning, as I reached for my phone to check the time, I saw a notification from Yahoo Messenger. My heart jumped. She had responded.

"Oh my goodness, it so good to hear from you again," she wrote. "I'm so glad to know you're okay. Rumors were seriously swirling here that you had killed yourself. A lot of people in Florida thought you were dead. I've been reading up on everything about the case, and I couldn't find any confirmation. I was so worried it was true. It's awesome and such a relief to know you're alive and okay. I'm definitely up for talking—we have a lot to catch up on. Write me anytime. I'm so glad you reached out. Hopefully I hear back from you soon."

Her response caught me off guard. For the first time in months, I felt something I hadn't felt in what seemed like forever—hope. Hope that there might be something beyond the pain, beyond the grief. I messaged her back, filling her in on everything that had happened, and our conversation began to flow effortlessly. When I asked why she had been online that night, she told me she had logged in to delete the account but saw me online and thought it might be a family member going through my things. She logged off, saddened by the thought. To me, it felt like more than coincidence.

As we talked, I began to see her in a new light. Our conversations before had been overshadowed by the chaos of my life with Jenny, and I realized we had never truly gotten to know each other. The more we talked, the more we discovered we had in common. It was unexpected but refreshing. I found myself drawn to her, feeling emotions I didn't think I was capable of anymore. These feelings gave me a renewed sense of purpose and energy—a much-needed reprieve from the darkness I had been living in.

But guilt wasn't far behind. Every time I felt myself growing closer to her, I couldn't help but feel like I was betraying Jenny's memory. It had only been six months since her passing, and the idea of moving on so fast just felt wrong. Those conflicting emotions became a constant struggle, but I couldn't deny the happiness and comfort she brought into my life.

Our conversations deepened over time, and eventually, we confessed our feelings we still had for each other.

It was uncharted territory for both of us, and I wasn't sure where it would lead. After a lot of thought I decided I had to know for sure this time. Without even discussing it, I surprised her with a flight to Tennessee, inviting her to spend a weekend with me. She was definitely surprised and completely caught off guard but ecstatic, and soon, she was on her way.

That weekend was nothing short of magical. We shopped around Opry Mills and walked around exploring the Opryland Hotel, talking and laughing like old friends rediscovering each other. For the first time in months, I felt alive again. But as the days turned into nights, the weight of my emotions became harder to ignore. Despite the growing connection between us, I couldn't bring myself to take things further. The guilt was too heavy, and I just wasn't ready. She understood, but it made those moments more difficult than either of us had anticipated.

When it was time for her to return to Florida, saying goodbye was harder than I expected. She confessed that she was falling for me all over again, and I admitted I feeling the same. As I watched her walk into the airport, tears in her eyes, I promised her we'd keep talking, even though I had no idea what the future held.

Not long after, she would take a leap of faith that changed everything, completely catching me off guard and drastically shifting the path of our lives forever. I was working a late-night shift, talking to my coworker Dave about her and how complicated things felt. As I explained my uncertainties, Dave replied, "You might want to start figuring that out," pointing to the window.

"Isn't that her?" he said.

There she was, standing outside with a packed car and her son in his car seat. She'd driven all the way from Florida to Tennessee with no intention of driving back. "I couldn't sit around any longer," she told me, wrapping her arms around me. "I'm falling in love with you, I know this is what I want, and I don't want to lose you again."

Her sudden move caught me off guard, but it also spoke volumes about her determination and the depth of her feelings. Without hesitation, I handed her my apartment keys and told her to head to my apartment and let herself in. I had no idea of what else to say or do. It was spontaneous, bold, and completely unexpected—but it felt right in the moment.

Living together from the start wasn't easy. We were thrown into the deep end, learning how to navigate our relationship while sharing a space and figuring out what our future might look like. There were challenges in the beginning—differences in communication, moments of doubt, and the weight of my lingering grief. But her optimism and commitment up front helped balance the uncertainty.

Her presence gave me a sense of purpose. She reminded me that life didn't have to be defined by loss. It was okay to move forward, to find joy in the present, and to build something new. She brought light into a life that had felt endlessly dark.

Her decision to take that leap pushed me to do the same emotionally. For so long, I had been stuck in a cycle of grief and self-doubt, but her boldness inspired me to let go of some of that fear. Slowly but surely, I started to rediscover parts of myself that I thought were lost.

Our relationship wasn't perfect, and there were moments when guilt and uncertainty crept in. But she displayed patience and understanding, helping me navigate those emotions. She'd remind me that healing was a process and that it's okay to take things one day at a time.

Her move to Tennessee marked a turning point in my journey. It wasn't just about starting a new relationship—it was about rebuilding my life. Her presence helped me find stability and hope at a time when I needed it most. She didn't erase the pain of the past, but she gave me a reason to look forward instead of behind me.

Looking back now, I realize how much her leap of faith mirrored what I needed to do emotionally. Her boldness and determination became a guiding light, showing me that sometimes the only way to heal is to take a chance—even if it feels scary or uncertain.

Shortly after she and I moved in together, things seemed to be going well on the surface. But it wasn't long before she began talking to me about marriage. She was very open about her desire to be married, believing it was the ultimate way to solidify our love and commitment. At first, our opinions differed. I wasn't sure we were ready, especially with how quickly everything was happening.

But amidst all the rapid decisions we were already making, I eventually agreed. I wanted to make her happy, and part of me thought that maybe this was the next step I needed to take to rebuild my life.

Soon after deciding, we went to the courthouse and got married. February 12th, 2010 we officially tied the knot. In the back of my mind, I knew we were moving way too fast, but the way I felt around her made me willing to ignore that voice of caution. What I knew, above all, was that I didn't feel the same overwhelming pain I had felt before she came back into my life. That was enough for me to say yes.

Unfortunately, the honeymoon phase didn't last long. Despite our romantic beginning—filled with butterflies and the rush of unexpected love—living together brought a new reality that quickly began to take its toll. For her, the challenges stemmed from her son and her son's father, who was understandably furious about her abrupt move to Tennessee. I hadn't personally taken any of that into consideration assuming she'd already had it all figured out. Their co-parenting relationship had already been tense, and this only made matters worse. Their disagreements escalated into a full-blown custody battle, which added a tremendous amount of stress to her life.

On my side, the grief and emotions I had pushed aside to focus on our relationship were still very much unresolved. I hadn't properly sorted through my feelings about Jenny's death, and it showed. She, on the other hand, who had been jealous of Jenny even before her passing, found herself questioning whether she could ever live up to what Jenny meant to me. That jealousy created insecurities in our marriage, which only added more strain.

The weight of these external pressures eventually began to clash with the internal struggles we were both facing. Arguments became more frequent, and the love that had once felt so full of hope began to feel like it was slipping through our fingers. The breaking point came when her custody battle required her to return to Florida for an extended period. The distance put our marriage on hold, and we had no idea how long it would take to resolve—or if our relationship could survive it.

When my wife left to go to Florida, I knew there was no guarantee of when she would be back. We were hopeful that the judge would decide in her favor quickly, but it didn't turn out that way. I tried my best to keep my head on straight while she was gone, but I had no idea this would become one of the most difficult periods of my life outside of losing Jenny. With my wife gone, I was left with a mix of worry and doubt, on top of having to face the remnants of everything I had tried so hard to avoid before. I was alone again, and this time with even more stress.

I tried to stay in close communication with my wife, but as time went on, that communication began to fade. My work schedule, her parenting responsibilities, and the demands of court started to clash, and with less communication arose more insecurity—but this time, more so on my side. The less I was able to talk to her, the more I worried that something might be wrong. All the emotional distress I had buried was coming to the surface, attaching itself to this newfound insecurity. Insecurity led to jealousy, jealousy led to questioning, and questioning led to arguments. That's exactly what happened.

Our conversations turned into a cycle of tension and conflict, eventually dwindling down altogether. I was at a loss, feeling horrible and overwhelmed. My emotions were all over the place. Deep down, I knew I still wasn't over what had happened with Jenny, and I felt guilty for rushing into such a deep relationship and eventual marriage so quickly. And now, my wife—who I'd been falling in love with and building so much hope for the future with—was stuck in Florida, and we weren't getting along.

Little did I know that our lack of communication would soon become the least of my problems. Before long, I received accusations about my wife that hit me like a ton of bricks. Her son's father would message me on FaceTime claiming that they were sleeping together and that she had been cheating on me all along since returning to Florida. I was shattered. I couldn't believe that after everything I had gone through, and everything my wife knew about my past, she could do something like that—let alone so soon after we got married.

I was completely broken. Dealing with everything I had avoided, now coupled with this betrayal, was just too much. After some time, I finally confronted her. I hoped—prayed, even—that she would deny it, that she would have proof that it wasn't true. Instead, I got the exact opposite. She admitted to it. There was just too much evidence to deny. But what hurt even more was her complete lack of remorse. She was cold, as cold as you could be. There were excuses sprinkled here and there, but the damage was already done.

The woman I had married, the person I had placed so much hope in for a brighter future, had shattered that hope in the worst way. Something in me clicked during a few conversations we had after the confrontation. It was as if all my emotions shut down and were somehow turned off. The tears dried up, and the questions stopped. I responded to her coldness with a coldness of my own, one I didn't even know I was capable of. I told her exactly what I thought of her, in the harshest possible way that I could. I told her to file for divorce while she was already in court because I was done. I hung up the phone on her, convinced it would be the last time I ever spoke to my wife.

But I couldn't have been more wrong.

CHAPTER 10

CROSSING BOUNDARIES

As time passed, I found myself grappling with a level of depression I had never experienced before. My wife's betrayal was inexcusable, and deep down, I knew I deserved better. But despite my best efforts to move forward and stand firm in my decision to divorce, the pain and doubt remained relentless. My head and my heart were a mess, tangled in emotions I was ill-equipped to handle.

I threw myself into distractions, desperately trying to numb the pain. Smoking, which had already become a bad habit, became constant. Then came the drinking. It started as weekends out with friends—club-hopping and getting drunk enough to forget everything. But soon, the weekends weren't enough. Weekdays began to blur into the mix, and I stopped caring about sleep. It wasn't like I was sleeping well anyway. I wanted to be anywhere but alone with my thoughts.

On one of those nights out, I would meet a girl who would eventually become a very important part of my life and change the direction of my life forever. It was through a close friend, who was my go-to for nights out in Antioch. We were at a local bar grabbing some food before heading to Silverados, one of the spots we frequented. A friend of his was also there with some of her friends. When my friend introduced us, she was undeniably attractive, with an easy confidence about her. I instinctively flirted with her lightly, but in my head, I already decided I shouldn't take it further. She was from Antioch, and I had a history with Antioch girls —a history that hadn't ever ended well.

Later that night, though, her and her friends showed up at Silverados too after we all had a few drinks. We ended up talking again, and this time, the conversation flowed more naturally. Conversation would lead to a few dances, and I found myself enjoying her company more than I expected. By the end of the night, I felt like I had surprisingly made a connection with her, even though I wasn't looking for anything serious.

Soon after, what started as casual meetups quickly became a regular thing. She and I began going out together often—

dancing, drinking, and just escaping the monotony of life. Before long, she started coming home with me after those nights out. At first, I didn't think much of it. To me, it was just a way to fill the emptiness. But as time went on, she became more involved in my life, and it turned into casual dating. Even though I knew deep down I wasn't emotionally available, I didn't stop it. I was enjoying spending my time with her and I needed and wanted the distraction.

At this time, it was no secret that she was fully back with her ex and was supposedly working on finalizing our divorce. The conversations I had with her were strictly about the divorce process, and she made it clear that she was moving forward in her relationship with her son's father. For me, that meant dating someone else wasn't wrong—I believed I was just waiting for the paperwork to be finalized. But when I wasn't out drinking or surrounded by people, the conflict inside me became impossible to ignore.

I was still mourning Jenny. I was still deeply in love with my wife, even though I was trying to move past the pain of her betrayal. And now, I was beginning a relationship with a woman that deserved more than I knew I could give her emotionally. It was chaos in my mind, and I felt like I was losing control.

Then came the night she dropped a bombshell—she told me she was pregnant and I was going to be a father. The words hit me like a freight train. I couldn't deny that I had been reckless and careless, but that didn't make it any easier to hear. My first thought wasn't excitement or even fear—it was disbelief. I didn't feel ready in any way. Emotionally, I was a wreck. Financially, I wasn't in a stable position. And physically, I was exhausted from everything I had been putting myself through.

Her revelation added another layer to the mess I was already in. Soon after, she confessed she was falling in love with me and wanted to talk about the possibility of building a family together. Her vulnerability left me feeling even worse. I couldn't give her what she wanted in the moment and I knew it. I knew I wasn't in love with her, and no matter how hard I tried to convince myself otherwise, those feelings just weren't there as much as I wished they would be. The guilt of not being able to offer her the love she deserved was overwhelming. It hurt and I hated myself for it.

As much as I didn't want to hurt her and I knew she didn't deserve it, I chose to be honest with her. I told her everything—about my wife, about my unresolved grief, and about the emotional state I was in. To her credit, she handled it far better than I expected. She didn't give up hope entirely, but she understood where I was coming from. We agreed to focus on co-parenting, knowing that a proper relationship between us likely wasn't in the cards for us anytime soon.

Around this time, I realized I needed to inform my wife. I called her and laid everything on the table. I told her I was still in love with her but shattered by what she had done. I told her how much hope I had placed in our marriage and how devastated I was that we couldn't make it work. Then, I told her about my new relationship and the pregnancy. I made it clear that I intended to dedicate myself fully to my child and that we needed to finalize our divorce. Her response was a quiet, disappointed "Okay," and that was it.

For a while, I immediately threw myself into preparing for fatherhood. I did everything I could to support my girlfriend during the pregnancy, even though I knew my feelings hadn't changed. I wanted to be present for our baby, even if I knew couldn't offer their mother the love she deserved. Then, unexpectedly, my wife called. She said she needed to come get the rest of her things. I was hesitant, knowing how I still felt about her, but I agreed.

Her visit reignited old emotions. Despite everything, we reconnected. I let my guard down, and it wasn't long before we fell back into old patterns. She apologized and made a multitude of excuses for her actions, and though I knew better, I forgave her. She told me she still loved me, wanted to work on our marriage and stay together. I reluctantly agreed, hoping desperately that it might fix everything.

Things became even more complicated soon after reconciling. My wife revealed that she was pregnant and I couldn't have been more twisted in my emotions. A doctor's conception estimate later confirmed the timing, making it clear that the baby was likely mine. In later discussions regarding the complications of our situation, it was rumored that my girlfriend had been with her ex during the beginning of our relationship as well. She denied the allegations and remained certain that her baby was mine but it definitely made things more difficult for me in the moment. I was stuck in a nightmare, completely unsure of how to move forward.

I tried my best to stay honest with both women. My girlfriend, however, didn't believe my wife's baby was mine. She insisted it was her ex's. My wife, on the other hand, was adamant that her baby was mine and later provided proof to back up her claims. Meanwhile, my girlfriend started leaning toward moving to D.C. to live with her mother and avoid the chaos our situation was becoming. Eventually she would move and the distance would make my decision a bit easier. If she wasn't going to stay, there was little keeping me in Tennessee. With very little control over either situation and my now ex girlfriend relocating to her mother's, I ultimately decided to move to Florida and give my marriage one last chance.

I sold everything I owned, gave away what I couldn't sell, and put in my two weeks' notice at work. When my lease expired, I packed up and headed to Florida, hoping for a fresh start. But deep down, I knew this move was filled with uncertainty—and that terrified me.

At first, things felt promising after I moved to Florida and reunited with my wife. We were riding the high of actually following through with our decision to stay married and rebuild, but there were still plenty of nerves simmering just below the surface. The uncertainty surrounding my ex girlfriend's pregnancy loomed large in my mind. If her baby turned out to be mine, it would create an incredibly complicated and painful situation for everyone involved, especially considering she was now in Washington, D.C., and I was in Florida. On the other hand, I couldn't help but wonder—what if the doctor had been wrong? What if my wife's baby wasn't mine after all? These questions spun around in my head constantly, making it nearly impossible to feel completely at ease.

On top of that, the stress of finding jobs and establishing financial stability added to the weight of everything we were trying to navigate. Despite our disagreements, I made an effort to stay in contact with my ex girlfriend and keep up with everything that was happening on her end. It wasn't always easy—our conversations sometimes turned contentious, and the tension made communication difficult at times. I tried my best to maintain a balance, being respectful to my wife while also ensuring I was there for my ex girlfriend as much as I could be, knowing she might be carrying my child. It was a delicate line to walk, and I often felt like I was failing at managing it all.

Looking back, I was angry with myself for creating such a chaotic situation—for myself, for my wife, for my ex girlfriend, and for the innocent children who were potentially involved. I had allowed my emotions to lead me down a path so unlike anything I'd ever imagined for myself, and the reality of it all was deeply upsetting. Still, I did what

I could to take things one day at a time and focus on moving forward.

Fortunately, some things began falling into place quickly, easing the burden. My wife and I both found jobs soon after I arrived in Florida, which helped to stabilize our situation. I started working as a store manager at Auntie Anne's. While it wasn't my first choice by any means, it offered better pay than I'd earned before, which was a relief. She got a position as a receptionist at an apartment complex, which was also a good start for her. With our financial concerns lessening, we began to settle into our new life together.

My wife had already done a lot of preparation before I arrived, which made the transition much smoother than I expected. I thought I'd be walking into an empty apartment, but to my surprise, my wife had furnished the place and made it feel like a home. It was a thoughtful gesture that made me feel more at ease in this new chapter of our lives.

Her family was another unexpected source of comfort. They knew about much of the chaos surrounding our marriage and the challenges we faced, but they were nothing but welcoming and supportive. Their kindness helped make the transition from Tennessee to Florida, and into this new phase of our marriage, feel a little less daunting.

As time went by and my wife and I settled into our new life in Florida, I tried to be as supportive as possible throughout her pregnancy. I was there for every appointment, craving, late-night Target run, and emotional moment she experienced. After all the sacrifices we had made to get to this point, I wanted nothing more than to return to normalcy and focus on enjoying our growing family. The more time passed, the more I found myself falling deeply in love with my wife again. Trust began to rebuild between us, and it finally felt like we were starting to put the past behind us while committing to handle the challenges in front of us together.

Both my ex girlfriend and my wife's due dates were drawing closer by the day, and the weight of the situation was becoming heavier. I couldn't help but worry that if my ex girlfriend's daughter turned out to be mine, I wouldn't be there for her delivery. The thought haunted me. These children were completely innocent, and I wanted to give them both the best I could. But the reality of the situation left me fearing that one child might inevitably receive less from me than the other.

My ex girlfriend was the first to go into labor. She delivered a healthy baby girl and although I wasn't there, I stayed updated about the baby through family members who were close to to my ex girlfriend. It wasn't long before I started hearing comments from everyone—"She looks just like you." When the first pictures reached me, my heart sank. As much as I wanted to believe there was still some uncertainty, I knew immediately deep down that her daughter was mine. The resemblance was undeniable. I was devastated. The realization that I couldn't be there to welcome her into the world cut deeply.

The pictures began circulating on social media, fueling gossip and swirling rumors. Nothing had been officially proven yet, as we hadn't done a paternity test, but the resemblance between my ex girlfriend's baby and me left little room for any doubt. Everyone knew it, including me and my wife and we couldn't avoid the truth any longer.

After my my daughter's mother had settled back home, I made a point to reassure her that I would take full responsibility. I promised her that once the paternity test confirmed what we already suspected, I would set up child support and do everything I could to be there for my daughter. Despite my efforts, tension between my daughter's mother and I would continue to grow. She had every right to feel the way she did, and I couldn't blame her. I had put all of us in a difficult position, and there didn't seem to be a solution that wouldn't hurt someone.

As the tension with my daughter's mother increased, communication between us began to break down. Our disagreements and the growing weight of the situation made it nearly impossible to maintain a positive connection. At a loss, I knew I had to shift my focus back to my wife and the baby we were also expecting together.

One night, after dinner, my wife's water broke unexpectedly. My heart raced as I rushed her to the hospital, calling her family on the way. When we arrived, everything happened so quickly. Before we knew it, my wife had delivered a healthy baby girl, and I stayed by her side the entire time. I cut the umbilical cord, tears welling in my eyes. But deep down, as much as I tried to stay in the moment, I found myself praying. I prayed to God that my wife's baby was mine. I knew our lives couldn't handle any more complications. With my ex girlfriend's baby almost certainly being mine, the thought of my wife's baby not being mine too was unbearable.

As the doctor handed me the newborn, I felt a nervous weight settle in my chest. I had never held a newborn baby before, and my arms shook as I cradled her tiny frame. I stared closely at her face, searching for something familiar. My heart sank. I tried to hide my devastation, but I knew deep down that my wife's baby wasn't mine. The truth hit me like a freight train, and though I held her gently in my arms, I felt like my entire world was falling apart again.

As time went by and the babies began to mature, their features became more distinctive. My ex girlfriend's daughter, every day, began to look more and more like me. On the other side of things, the exact opposite was happening with my wife's daughter. Deep down, I had known the truth from the very first moment I held her in the hospital. But now, others were starting to see it too—my wife's family, her friends, and even acquaintances. My wife's daughter bore a striking resemblance to her ex, the same man she had cheated on me with and who she'd been with just before our reconciliation.

This was an extremely difficult reality for both of us, but it was a topic neither my wife nor I were ready to face directly. We avoided it for as long as we could, but eventually, the resemblance became undeniable. I decided it was time to confront the truth and approached my wife about the paternity of her daughter. She did not take it well. The conversation immediately turned heated, as she was visibly upset that I was even bringing it up.

I told her honestly that I believed there was a great chance her daughter wasn't mine biologically and that we needed to do the right thing for everyone involved. She did not agree. Over time, we had several conversations about the subject, none of which ended well. It felt like we were constantly circling the same point, both of us unwilling to fully face the implications. My ex girlfriend's daughter was undeniably mine, and my wife's daughter was almost certainly not—but we were at a stalemate. The truth hovered between us, a weight neither one of us could ignore.

I was beginning to come to terms with it all and wanted to address it head-on. In my mind, getting the paternity test and revealing the truth wasn't the end of our marriage. It was simply the right thing to do for everyone involved—most importantly, for the children. My wife, however, did not see it that way. She expressed numerous times that she didn't want to get a paternity test. As much as I believed she knew the truth, she remained in denial for months, and this only added to the tension between us.

Eventually, my wife admitted what I had suspected all along. The resemblance was undeniable. She also felt strongly that her daughter was not mine. Despite this admission, she stood firm in her decision not to get a paternity test. She explained her reasoning to me, saying she didn't want to go through the same ordeal she had experienced with her son. She feared that if her ex was confirmed as the father, he would gain some form of control over her daughter's life—and by extension, over our marriage. She didn't want to risk that, and I could tell the idea terrified her.

While I understood where she was coming from and empathized with her concerns, I still wholeheartedly disagreed. I couldn't lie to this baby. She deserved to know who her real father was, and I stood firmly by that belief. The clash between our perspectives created a growing divide in our marriage. The trust and connection we had worked so hard to rebuild began to crumble under the weight of this unresolved conflict. Old wounds that we thought had healed started to reopen, dragging us back to the very same issues that had broken us in the first place.

Time went by, and we transitioned into a new apartment, rooming with my wife's best friend at the time. This decision was made to save money since things weren't working out with my wife's job, and she wanted to step back into being a stay-at-home mother again. Despite our strong attempts to move forward and put the past behind us, the tension between us remained thick. The disagreements weren't always directly about the children or paternity, but because those unresolved issues lingered, even the smallest disagreements would escalate into full-blown arguments. These conflicts were growing more consistent over time, and the strain they created was palpable.

Adding to the tension, I was wrestling with my own personal guilt. My daughter was states away from me, and not being able to be there for her was eating me alive. I constantly questioned myself as a father, wondering if I was doing enough and if I'd made the right decisions. So when my wife would argue with me—whether it was about paternity or something entirely unrelated—I couldn't help but think, Where's the appreciation for the sacrifices I've made and continue to make? I felt like I was giving everything I had to hold things together, while sacrificing building a strong relationship with my daughter but it didn't seem to be enough. All I wanted was to do the right thing, but the weight of everything was suffocating.

Living with my wife's friend didn't make things any easier for me. Whenever my wife and I had disagreements, it often felt like her friend would team up with her, leaving me feeling outnumbered and isolated. It was an uncomfortable situation all around, but I tried my best to make it work for the sake of our family.

As time went by, I buried my focus into my job, hoping for some kind of breakthrough—a raise or a promotion that might alleviate some of the stress. Luckily, I eventually got the promotion I had been working toward, but it wasn't enough to solve our deeper issues. Things would eventually come to a head and my wife would be caught cheating again, this time for the third time. With undeniable evidence presented to her, she had no choice but to gather her belongings and leave. In the process, she stranded me and her friend in the apartment with nowhere to go, as our lease was only halfway through its term.

As time went by, my wife and I transitioned into a new phase of life, albeit apart. I was trying to rebuild from the wreckage she had left behind, but the challenges seemed endless. Living in Florida, stranded with my wife's best friend as a roommate while my wife herself had not only been caught cheating again, but she'd moved back in with her children's father—the same man she cheated on me with for the third time— it was chaotic beyond words. Every day felt like an emotional hurricane.

I thought I had reached the limit of what I could handle until one payday when I noticed my paycheck was significantly lighter. Checking my account, I saw child support deductions. Confused and alarmed, I immediately contacted my daughter's mother, thinking perhaps she had initiated something prematurely, though paternity for her daughter hadn't been determined. She adamantly denied any involvement, leaving me with only one possibility: My wife?

I contacted child support services, and my worst suspicions were confirmed. My wife had voluntarily put me on child support for her daughter—the one we knew wasn't biologically mine. She had done this while living with the biological father of that child, forcing me to pay for a child she knew wasn't mine. I was disgusted—not just with her, but with myself for allowing this chaos to overtake my life.

My emotions were spiraling out of control. Everywhere I turned, I felt the weight of poor decisions and emotional instability piling on top of me. I couldn't see a way out.

Whether at work or home, I was consumed by frustration, regret, and disbelief. Desperate for an outlet, I began confiding in coworkers who soon became close friends. These relationships became my lifeline, providing me a reprieve from the turmoil.

Outside of work, I spent more time with these friends, which gave me something to look forward to and helped to distract me from the mess I was living in. When my wife's friend finally moved out of our shared apartment, one of my coworkers stepped up to help me keep the place. This simple act lifted a massive weight off my shoulders. For the first time in months, I felt like I could breathe just a little.

But my wife's presence, even from a distance, continued to haunt me. She had fully recommitted to her relationship with her children's father, leaving me to pick up the pieces of our shattered marriage while paying child support for their child. It was an inescapable injustice I couldn't even afford to fight in court. No matter how many calls I made or how much I protested, without a paternity test, there was nothing I could do and she knew it.

During this time, I began drinking heavily again. While I wasn't drinking as heavily as I had in 2009, it was still enough to be concerning. My nights out with friends, though fun, were becoming a crutch. It was during this period that I grew closer to a girl I had hired months earlier at work. She was someone I respected and admired professionally, and though she was undeniably attractive and exactly my type, I had always maintained a professional and respectful relationship with her.

However, as we spent more time together outside of work with our friend group, I found myself more drawn to her. We clicked naturally, sharing similar interests, and I began to like her on a deeper level. The casual conversations soon turned into flirtation, and it became clear there was something between us.

The situation was complicated by one of my close friends, who had also shown interest in her. Out of respect, I held back, but eventually, he approached me and encouraged me to pursue her, believing she might be into me. His blessing removed the hesitation I had felt before.

One night, after a group outing, we ended up back at my place. As the night wound down and friends started leaving, she stayed behind with me to continue on conversation. We talked for hours, opening up about life, struggles, and everything in between. I admitted I found myself starting to really like her but also shared my reluctance to rush into anything serious given my recent history. She listened, understanding and compassionate, which only deepened my interest in her.

Out of respect, I offered her a place to sleep on the couch rather than letting her drive home late at night. She agreed, and I headed to bed. But just as I was drifting off to sleep, I got a text on my phone. "Are you asleep?" she'd wrote and before I could reply I heard my bedroom door open.

That night would begin a short-lived relationship that would bring out a side of my wife I had never seen before—a side I didn't think she was capable of, a side that truly scared me.

As time went by, my relationship with the girl from work began to grow. We started spending more time together, hanging out regularly, and she would occasionally stay the night. I really enjoyed her company and felt like there might be something worth exploring between us. From the very beginning, I had been upfront and honest with her about the chaos in my life, and it felt good to have someone who understood and still wanted to give our connection a chance. For the first time in a while, I felt like I could see a potential path forward, even if it was far from perfect.

Unfortunately, that hope would be short-lived. One morning, after she had stayed the night, everything changed for the worse. I had to work early, while she didn't have to be in until later that day, so I told her she could sleep in. Since my roommate was home, he could let her out when she was ready to leave. It seemed like a simple plan, but what happened next completely blindsided me.

While I was busy opening the store, my phone started blowing up. At first, I couldn't answer because I was juggling tasks, but the rapid succession of calls—from her, then my roommate, and then my wife—immediately told me something was wrong. I called my roommate back, and his panicked voice confirmed it.

"You need to come home now," he said. "Your ex just broke into the apartment and tried to attack us with a knife."

I was stunned. "What? Are you serious? What happened?"

"She busted through your bedroom window. There's blood everywhere—she cut herself climbing through the glass. Then she grabbed a knife and came after us. I had to tackle her to knock it out of her hand. When I said I was calling the cops, she ran out."

I couldn't believe what I was hearing. I asked if everyone was okay. He assured me that they was shaken up but unharmed and insisted I get home immediately because the police were on their way. My mind raced as I tried to process what had just happened.

On my way home, my wife called me. I answered, demanding to know what she was thinking. She immediately began screaming unintelligibly at the top of her lungs. I couldn't make out most of what she was saying, just a stream of anger, cursing, and distorted words. I tried to calm her down, but it was no use. Frustrated and overwhelmed, I hung up and focused on getting home.

When I walked into the apartment, the scene was surreal. My roommate and the girl from work were visibly shaken, and the apartment looked like something out of a crime show. Blood was smeared across the walls and bed, with shattered glass scattered on the floor. There were muddy footprints on the bed where my wife had jumped across it, and shards of glass glinted in the sunlight. It was chaos.

I checked on the girl I'd been seeing first, asking if she was okay. She nodded, but the fear and disbelief were evident on her face. "You need to tell the cops everything," she said firmly. "What she did was dangerous. This isn't okay Keith."

I agreed but could see the toll it had already taken on her. She left shortly after, and my roommate stayed a little longer to walk me through what had happened. The more he explained, the more surreal it felt. My wife had literally shattered the window, climbed through the glass, and lunged at her with a knife. It was something I never imagined she was capable of, and it terrified me.

When the police arrived, they were just as shocked by the scene. They told me I could press charges but explained that without direct testimony from the others, it might not hold up. They advised me to get some form of security for the apartment and consider filing a restraining order. After speaking with my roommate and the girl from work, it became clear neither of them wanted to get further involved. They were justified in their hesitation, and I understood.

I texted my wife later that day, telling her that what she did was inexcusable. I warned her that if she ever showed up at my property unannounced again, I would press charges without hesitation. I also reminded her to think about her kids and what would happen if she were arrested. She never responded.

Cleaning up the mess—both physically and emotionally—was draining. I replaced the window and did my best to move forward, but the damage was done. The girl I had been seeing from work understandably distanced herself, and any potential relationship we had fizzled out. The incident left me with a profound sense of unease and a realization of just how volatile things had become.

That night marked the end of something I had hoped would be a fresh start, and it left me questioning everything about the choices I had made and the path I was on.

My wife's actions during this time deeply affected my ability to move forward, especially when it came to trusting others or even considering the idea of a new relationship. After everything that happened, the thought of dating or even casually hanging out with another woman felt like too much of a risk. I didn't want to put anyone else in harm's way, nor did I want to risk my wife doing something reckless that could jeopardize her future or her role as a mother to her children. It just didn't make sense to me. Why would my wife react in such an extreme and irrational way if she had been the one who cheated, left, and was now living with her children's father? She had made it clear she had moved on—or so I thought. But the moment I tried to move forward with someone else, she did this? Why? That single question echoed in my mind, over and over. Why?

I couldn't wrap my head around it. There was no logic to it. She had barely communicated with me for months while living with the man she cheated on me with. Yet the second I attempted to build something new, she completely unraveled. It was as if she didn't want me, but she also didn't want anyone else to have me either. The whole situation left me confused and emotionally drained.

Despite all of this, I couldn't help but think about the girl from work. Though our time together had been cut short by my wife's actions, I still held her in high regard and wondered what could've been. I still see posts from her occasionally, showing the wonderful person and amazing mother she's become, and it makes me happy to see her thriving. Every now and then, I'll catch myself wondering "what if," and it stings a little, but I know that's water under the bridge. She deserves the happiness she's found, and I'm glad she's doing well.

In the aftermath of it all, I buried myself in work, trying to sort through my emotions and pull some semblance of positivity from the chaos. I started working out again, primarily running, and found solace in it. Running became my escape, my therapy. It helped me clear my head, and with it came a rediscovery of music. For a long time, I had avoided listening to music altogether because it brought too many painful reminders of everything I was trying to forget. Music had always been such a central part of my life, but during my darkest times, it only amplified the sadness and heartbreak.

But now, with running, I started listening to more uplifting and motivational tracks, and it began to reignite a light in me that I had lost. It didn't happen overnight, but little by little, I started feeling like myself again. The exercise and the music worked hand in hand to improve my mental health. It gave me something to focus on, something positive to hold onto.

Yet, no matter how far I ran or how much progress I made, there was one thing I just couldn't shake no matter how much time had passed. No matter how much I hated to admit it, I knew deep down I was still in love with my wife. And I hated myself for it. After everything she had done—after all the chaos and heartbreak she had caused—I knew I still loved her. It was a shame I carried heavily, a reminder that some wounds don't heal as easily as others.

Knowing deep down that I was still in love with her while also being so hurt and disgusted by the entire situation was a constant internal battle. It was a conflicting set of emotions that left me feeling lost, like I was constantly fighting myself. I couldn't understand for the life of me how, after everything she had done, I could still feel anything but anger toward her. There was no way in my mind that this could be healthy. Something had to be wrong. There had to be some kind of explanation for why my heart was clinging to her, despite all the pain she had put me through.

I tried everything I could to shake the feeling. I continued running and working out, doing whatever I could to focus my energy elsewhere. I hung out with friends as much as possible, but it was in those quiet moments—when I was home alone, driving to work, or lying in bed at night—that it would creep back in. The frustration always led me back to the same thought: If none of this had happened, if Jenny was still here, none of this would even be going on. The memories of Jenny would flood my mind, pulling me into an endless loop of regret, remorse, and what ifs. It was excruciating, and I hated myself for it.

The worst part of it all was that she knew. No matter how much I tried to hide it, there were subtleties in my demeanor, in my actions, in my hesitations that made it clear to her that I still cared. And because of that, she took every opportunity she could to worm her way back into my heart.

One night, I was home alone after work, taking a shower, when I heard the unmistakable sound of my bathroom door opening. That's not a sound anyone wants to hear when they're home alone—especially not when they're in the shower. My stomach sank, and I peeked around the curtain, bracing myself for the worst. But instead of an intruder, I saw my wife standing there, just smiling at me.

I froze. "What are you doing here? How did you even get in?"

She didn't answer. She just smirked at me, turned around, and walked toward the bedroom down the hall.

Still completely caught off guard and creeped out, I quickly finished rinsing off and wrapped a towel around myself. As I processed what had just happened, it hit me—I had never changed the locks, and she still had a key. With everything that had been going on, I had been too preoccupied to even think about it. She had let herself in while I was in the shower, knowing exactly how vulnerable I was.

I walked toward the bedroom, hesitant but needing answers. When I opened the door, there she was—laying on my bed, waiting for me. She'd let herself in with the intent to be with me.

"What are you doing?" I asked, already knowing the answer but still in disbelief that this was actually happening.

Again, she didn't answer. She just motioned for me to join her.

My mind was screaming at me to walk away. Every logical part of me knew this was a terrible idea. But my emotions, the ones I had been fighting so hard to suppress, had other plans. And she knew exactly how to win this battle. She knew she was attractive. She knew exactly what I was drawn to. She had made sure to spend extra time on herself before coming over, and it was working.

That night, my mind would lose to my emotions.

For those few hours, none of the pain, none of the betrayal, none of the chaos mattered. It was just me and her. We were husband and wife again. And for a moment, it felt like nothing had ever changed.

But as soon as it was over, the reality set in like a weight pressing down on both of us. There was no conversation. No attempt to justify what had just happened. She quietly got dressed and left my apartment without a word.

And I sat there, staring at the door after it closed behind her, thinking the same thing I had thought so many times before:

What has my life become?

Over a week passed without a single word between us after that night. As much as it had shocked me, I realized it must have shocked her just as much. No matter how I tried to rationalize it, I knew getting involved with her again was a bad idea. It didn't matter what emotions I was feeling—this was a mistake. I needed to stay away. I needed to figure out how to rid myself of these feelings that I still had for her.

As word traveled through our mutual connections in Florida, I learned that my wife had moved and was now living with her stepdad. I wondered if that had something to do with why she showed up that night, but in the end, it didn't change anything. It didn't justify what had happened, and it didn't make my feelings any less conflicted.

I tried to shift my focus elsewhere, pushing myself in the opposite direction. I wanted to be free of her hold on me. But as I worked to distance myself, my wife pulled in the opposite direction. The silence must have triggered something in her because, after a week of nothing, she started texting me. At first, it was small talk—little messages here and there that I ignored. But she knew how to push my buttons. She knew exactly how to reel me back in, and it wasn't long before our brief exchanges turned into full-length conversations.

She went from being polite, asking to pick up her things, to inviting me over to visit her at her stepdad's house. I still got along with her stepdad, which made the idea of visiting a little easier. But every time I left, I had the same thought—What am I doing? I told myself I wouldn't go back, but I always did. It felt too good to have her close again, even when I knew it was dangerous.

As we talked more seriously, I found myself opening up. I told her about my conflicted feelings, my reservations, and the battles I was fighting within myself over trusting her again. It was during these conversations that I decided to address something that had been looming in the background—what had happened at my apartment with the knife. That night, when she broke in through the window, covered in blood, and tried to attack the girl I was seeing—it wasn't something I could just ignore.

I asked her point-blank why she had done it, what had gone through her mind, and whether she had planned it or if it had just happened in the heat of the moment. She took a deep breath before answering. She told me that she had come over to get the rest of her things and hadn't expected to see someone else in my bed. She claimed that the sight of another woman in what used to be our space triggered something inside her that she wasn't even aware she was capable of. She swore it wasn't premeditated, that it was purely reactionary, and that she lost control in that moment. She apologized, swearing up and down that nothing like that would ever happen again. She also thanked me for not pressing charges after I explained that I hadn't done so for the sake of the kids.

Hearing her acknowledge what happened and take responsibility for it helped me to understand why it happened, but it didn't erase the fact that it did happen. A part of me still felt very uneasy. But another part of me—the part that knew I still loved her, that still wanted to believe she was capable of change—wanted to let it go.

She admitted that she didn't want a divorce, but she also revealed something that stunned me—while she had been staying with her stepdad, she had started seeing someone else. She had rekindled a relationship with an old friend from New York, a guy who had recently moved to Florida and had developed strong feelings for her.

I was floored. After everything, now there was another person involved? I couldn't wrap my head around it. She was telling me she wanted to stay married, while at the same time confessing that she had been seeing someone else. It was all too much. The chaos surrounding our marriage, the constant back and forth, the endless cycle of heartbreak—I didn't know how to process any of it.

That revelation put a stall to our communication again. I pulled away, trying to protect myself, but she wasn't about to let that happen. She knew exactly how to draw me back in, and once again, it worked. She ended things with the guy from New York and insisted that she wanted to work on our marriage. As much as I knew it was the wrong decision before I made it, as much as I knew I should've walked away, I eventually let her back in.

Looking back, it's clear to me now exactly what was happening. But back then, I had no idea. I had no experience with emotional manipulation. I had never felt these kinds of emotions before. My mind was at war with my heart, and for some reason, my heart always won when it came to her. It was like I was trapped in an endless storm of chaos, clinging to the decisions that hurt the least instead of the ones that made the most sense.

My wife and I would eventually move back in together, this time into a house with a mother-in-law suite in Jacksonville. Her stepfather, who worked most of the month out of town, agreed to let us rent the suite and split the cost when he was in town. It helped lessen our financial stress and allowed us to focus on trying to rebuild what was left of our marriage.

The kids were ecstatic. They were happy that we were back together, and I wanted so badly for that to be enough. I gave it a genuine effort. I really tried. But this time, I drew a firm line in the sand. I told her that if she ever did this again—if she ever betrayed me one more time—no matter how much I loved her, no matter how much it hurt, I would never let her back in. She promised me it would never happen again. A promise I desperately hoped she could keep.

It was a promise she would eventually break.

And when she did, it would lead to the last time I would ever live in Florida. It would lead me back to Nashville—a place I had spent years running from, a place I had promised myself I'd never return to. But when the time came, I wouldn't have a choice.

CHAPTER 11

BREAKING POINT

The last few weeks of my relationship with my wife in Florida felt off. Over the years, I had developed an instinct when it came to her—a gut feeling that told me when something wasn't right. Every time I had ignored it in the past, I ended up blindsided by the truth, and more often than not, it was worse than I ever could have imagined. This time was no different.

The feeling had been creeping up on me for weeks, and though I had tried to ignore it, I couldn't shake the anxiety in my gut. Then one day, while she was in the shower, I noticed her phone lighting up with messages. I hesitated. I didn't want to be this guy again—I didn't want to be the person checking his wife's phone, searching for proof of something I already knew deep down. But I couldn't resist. I picked up the phone, checked the messages, and there it was.

It was her ex.

They were flirting.

There weren't any explicit pictures or solid proof that they had been sleeping together this time, but I didn't need it. At this point, the flirtation alone was enough for me. It confirmed what my gut had already been screaming at me. I walked into the bathroom, phone in hand, and held up the messages in front of her.

She barely reacted.

The cold, distant look I had seen so many times before took over her face, and she stared at me as if I had just informed her about the weather. I told her she needed to leave—that she needed to get her things and go be with him, since that's clearly where she wanted to be. Without hesitation, she agreed. "Ok, I'll start packing," she said in an eerily calm voice, turning away as if this was just another normal day in our marriage.

As she gathered her belongings, I went outside to call my sister Bootsie, needing someone to talk to. I needed someone to reel me back in and keep me calm. That's when I noticed something that sent my blood boiling.

My wife had started loading some of my things into her car.

I had just bought an Xbox, and she was carrying it outside along with a stack of my games, loading them into the backseat. I walked over, still on the phone, and calmly grabbed the Xbox out of her hands.

"What do you think you're doing?" I asked.

She spun around, furious, and started throwing the games into the car, slamming the back door shut before I could grab them.

"Give me my stuff." I said, reaching for the door handle.

She shoved my arm away, yelling and cursing at me. When I reached again, she whipped out her keychain, lifted it up, and sprayed my face and everything else she could with mace.

The pain was immediate and excruciating. My eyes burned as if they were on fire, and within seconds, I couldn't see a thing. I dropped everything in my hands, stumbling back as the searing pain took over.

I heard her car door slam.

I heard her tires screech as she sped away.

I was left standing in the backyard, completely blind, gasping for air as the chemicals burned my skin.

I had to get inside.

I fumbled my way toward the back door, but it was locked. My keys were inside. I had no way to get in. My own wife—who had promised me just months before that she wanted to fix our marriage—had just maced me, stolen my things, and left me stranded in my own backyard.

Eventually, I somehow managed to break into the mother-in-law suite since her stepfather was out of town. I rushed to the sink, splashing cold water onto my face, but unfortunately it only made it worse. My skin felt like it was melting off. My eyes were swollen shut. I couldn't think, I couldn't breathe—I could only suffer.

Hours passed before the pain finally subsided enough for me to open my eyes again. I sat on the back porch, staring at the ground, furious with myself.

How did I let this happen again?

What kind of idiot was I to believe she could possibly change?

Why couldn't I just stop loving her?

I hated myself for falling into the same cycle, over and over again. I knew, without a doubt, that this was it. I had to end it. I had to leave Florida. I had to get as far away from her as possible if I ever wanted to break free.

I picked up my phone and called my sister again. She had just moved back home to Nashville with her family, and I knew if anyone could help me figure this out, it was her. I told her everything—about my wife's infidelity, the constant manipulation, and now, her outright assault. Bootsie listened to every word and didn't hesitate.

"Keith, you need to come home."

She offered to buy me a ticket out, but I told her I could manage it myself. I just needed to line a few things up first. I made some calls, found a way back into the house to grab my things, and packed up as much as I could fit in my car. Before I left, I sat down at the kitchen table and wrote my wife a letter.

I told her I was done.

I told her I had loved her more than anything, that I had always wanted better for our marriage than this. But it wasn't enough. It had never been enough. I reminded her of all the times I had forgiven her, of all the second chances, of all the broken promises. I told her that this was the last time.

I folded up the note, placed my wedding band on top of it, and left it on the table.

Then, without looking back, I got into my car and headed home.

Returning to Nashville felt like stepping back into a past I had spent years trying to escape. This city held too many memories, too much pain, and an overwhelming sense of failure. But after what happened with my wife, I knew I had no choice. I had to leave Florida, and I had to finally let her go.

Since I left late at night, I called my sister Leeanne, who was living in Georgia at the time. I explained everything—my wife's latest betrayal, the mace, the final breaking point that led me to finally walk away. She listened without judgment and invited me to stop in Georgia before heading home to Tennessee. I was grateful. The thought of going straight back to Nashville felt unbearable, and having a buffer, even for a few days, was a much-needed relief.

On my way to Leeanne's, I called my daughter's mother. I wanted her to know where things stood with me and my wife and that I was coming back to Nashville for good. To my surprise, she told me that things in D.C. weren't working out for her either, and she was considering moving back to Tennessee too. The more we talked, the more it made sense. If we were both in Nashville, it would make it easier for me to be present in my daughter's life. She had always wanted that for our daughter, and for the first time, it seemed like we were both on the same page.

By the time I arrived at Leeanne's house, My daughter's mother had already made her decision—she was moving back to Nashville, too. The timing felt surreal. We hadn't planned this together, but somehow, life had aligned us back in the same place. My sister welcomed us both, and for a short while, it was nice to feel like I was back in a familiar, safe space.

Being with my daughter again after so much time apart was overwhelming in the best way. She had grown so much, and I hated how much I had missed. During those few days in Georgia, I soaked up every second I could with her, making up for lost time in the only way I knew how—just being there.

At night, when everyone else had gone to bed, My daughter's mother and I found ourselves talking for hours. We had been through so much together, and despite our rocky past, there was still a level of comfort between us that was hard to ignore. We talked about everything—our daughter, our regrets, our frustrations, and the unexpected turns our lives had taken. Those late-night conversations led to something I didn't anticipate. We fell into old habits and it happened more than once. Though we both knew it was a mistake, we let it happen anyway.

For my daughter's mother, it reignited feelings she had tried to suppress for years. For me, it brought nothing but guilt. I had spent so long feeling broken over my wife, and now, here I was, making choices that only seemed to complicate things further. But if there was one thing I never did with my daughter's mother, it was lie. I told her the truth—about my feelings, my doubts, my confusion. I reassured her that I wanted to be in my daughter's life, but I couldn't give her false hope again that we would ever be a family. She understood, and to her credit, she didn't hold it against me.

Eventually, it was time to head back to Nashville. My daughter's mother and I packed our cars and made the drive separately, knowing that while we were heading to the same place, we weren't heading there together.

Returning to my hometown was surreal. It was the last place I wanted to be, but the only place I had left. My sister Bootsie had recently moved back from California, and she had offered me a place to stay. But as we talked through the logistics, we realized it probably wasn't the best fit.

Bootsie's family didn't smoke, and I was still deep in my habit. While she made it known that I was still welcome, the last thing I wanted was to impose.

That's when my mom offered me a room at her apartment. The thought made my stomach turn. The last thing I wanted was to step back into a space filled with childhood memories I had spent my life trying to outrun. But she had the room, and she smoked, which meant I could, too. In the end, it was the more logical option, even if it wasn't what I wanted.

I unloaded my car, carried my bags inside, and stepped into the room that still held my old furniture and remnants of my past. I shut the door behind me, turned off the lights, and laid down on the bed—staring at the ceiling, lost in thought.

I had left this city with so much hope for my future. I had built a life with someone I thought I would spend forever with. I had loved and lost in ways I never thought possible. And now, after everything, I was right back where I started.

I felt like a failure.

The weight of it all crushed me. I wanted to close my eyes and never wake up. But when I did, I saw my daughter's face. And that image alone reignited a fire inside me that I hadn't felt in years.

I made myself a promise that night.

If I couldn't be anything else in this world, I was going to be the greatest father I could be.

That was the only thing keeping me moving forward.

Adjusting to my new reality in Nashville wasn't easy. I had spent so much time running from my past, trying to build something new, only to end up right back where I started. I never wanted to come back home, and I could barely stand to visit, but I knew I had no other option. The only way forward was to put my head down and focus on what mattered most—my daughter.

In order to be the best father I could be, I needed to get my head on straight and start making strides financially. My mom had offered me a place to stay for as long as I needed, and I decided to take advantage of that stability while I figured things out. The first step was securing unemployment, which thankfully was granted. It provided me with some financial relief, giving me a little breathing room to plan my next move.

I wasted no time applying for jobs, casting a wide net with applications to any place that was hiring—but I was adamant about one thing: I refused to work anywhere in Antioch. The memories there were suffocating, and the last thing I needed was to be constantly reminded of the past I was trying to move forward from. Most of my time was spent job-hunting online, but any free time I had was devoted to my daughter and maintaining a positive relationship with her mother.

My daughter's mother had brought up the idea of us possibly moving in together multiple times, framing it as a way to co-parent under one roof. On the surface, it made sense, but I knew exactly how that would play out. I wasn't naïve. Living together would create a slippery slope that neither of us was ready for, and forcing something that wasn't there naturally would only lead to more complications. I was upfront with her about where I stood. I wanted to be the best father possible and build a solid co-parenting foundation, but I wasn't ready to jump back into a situation that could implode at any moment.

As time passed, my job search wasn't yielding any results, and being stuck at my mom's apartment in Antioch was beginning to weigh on me mentally. I felt like I was trapped, like I was regressing instead of progressing. I had multiple conversations with Bootsie about it, and she reminded me over and over that her door was open if I needed a change. Eventually, I decided to take her up on the offer. She lived in Cool Springs, and I knew Franklin and Brentwood had far more job opportunities than I was finding in Nashville.

Moving in with my older sister would require a major adjustment. The biggest challenge? I would have to quit smoking. Anyone who has ever tried to quit smoking understands how brutal it can be, and I had been a heavy smoker for years. But I knew this was an opportunity to reframe my mindset and challenge myself to become better, both mentally and physically. I decided to channel my energy into fitness, setting a goal to get into the best shape of my life. If I could push through the withdrawal, push through the cravings, and replace those moments of weakness with running and working out, I knew I could break the habit.

With a new environment, a new challenge, and the opportunity for a fresh start waiting for me, I finally felt something I hadn't felt in a long time—hope.

Moving in with Bootsie turned out to be one of the best decisions I could have made at that time. She had always been a positive light in my life—someone who carried an unshakable optimism, no matter how chaotic things got. Being around her made it easier to see the glass as half full, even when my mind wanted to see it as empty. She was someone I could always open up to, and she always had something uplifting to say in response. No matter what I was dealing with, I always felt better after talking to her.

My brother-in-law and nephew also helped make the transition easier. We had similar interests, whether it was sports or tech, and that gave me a refreshing distraction—

something to focus on that wasn't tied to stress, heartbreak, or the past. It was the first time in a long time that I felt like I could breathe.

As soon as I settled in, I started filling out job applications, determined to regain a sense of independence. Before long, I landed a management position at Wendy's in Cool Springs. It wasn't exactly what I had in mind for my next career move, but I needed a job, and they were offering stability and a solid paycheck. I took the opportunity without hesitation, knowing that getting back into a routine was crucial for my mental and financial well-being.

Surprisingly, I found myself enjoying the job more than I expected. The crew I worked with was welcoming, and we shared a lot of common interests. I quickly bonded with my coworkers, which helped me build friendships outside of my family. Having people to talk to, joke around with, and even text outside of work made a huge difference. It gave me a sense of normalcy I hadn't felt in a long time.

Between working, spending time with my daughter, and working out, I finally felt like things were starting to come together. Slowly but surely, I was regaining a sense of self.

The weight of everything I had gone through still lingered, but for the first time in a while, it didn't feel like it was suffocating me.

Bootsie also encouraged me to start going to church again, and I decided to give it another shot. We began attending World Outreach Church in Murfreesboro, and from the very first sermon, I felt something different. I had tried church before—many times, in many places—but I never truly connected with it the way I did here. The way the preacher delivered his messages resonated with me in a way that felt personal, as if he was speaking directly to me and the things I had been struggling with. The more I went, the more I felt like I was healing in ways I hadn't even realized I needed to heal. It gave me clarity, peace, and—most importantly—a sense of direction.

This newfound sense of positivity in my life started to build up a strength inside of me that I had been missing for years. For so long, I had felt stuck, lost in cycles of heartbreak, mistakes, and self-doubt. But now, for the first time in my adult life, I started looking ahead—not just for survival, but for something greater.

And with that realization came a decision that would change everything: I was going to take the next step and do something I had never done before.

I was going to live alone. For the first time ever, I was going to have my own place—just for me.

As I started looking for apartments, a mix of emotions weighed heavily on me. The idea of living alone for the first time was both exciting and terrifying. I had spent so many years bouncing between relationships, heartbreak, and temporary living arrangements that the thought of having a space that was completely mine felt surreal. But with that came an unsettling realization—this was truly all on me. No more crutches, no more fallback plans, no more distractions.

I knew there were so many mental and emotional issues I had yet to fully address, and the thought of being alone with them concerned me. I had battled depression for years, and I worried that the silence of an empty apartment might make those feelings creep back in. Would I spiral? Would I find myself trapped in my thoughts again, unable to move forward? These were questions I couldn't answer, but they loomed over me like a shadow.

Despite the fear, I tried to focus on the positives. This was my chance to truly move forward. I thought about the excitement of building a real home for myself, a place where I could finally feel settled. More than anything, I thought about my daughter and how this would give us a space to grow together. The idea of creating a home for her, where she would have her own room, her own space to visit and make memories with me—it gave me a newfound sense of purpose. I wanted to make this work, not just for myself, but for her.

The more I thought about all the possibilities, the more my confidence grew. My mindset shifted from fear to determination. I had family and friends rooting for me, offering support and encouragement every step of the way. It felt like, for the first time in a long time, things were actually aligning in the right direction.

Then one morning, I woke up and as I reached for my phone, I noticed one missed call and an unread text message. It was my wife.

"Hey, I just wanted to see how you were doing. We miss you, I miss you"

And instantly, all of the unresolved emotions began to resurface.

It had gotten to the point over time where the thought of her no longer gave me butterflies but instead left a sinking feeling in my gut. There had been so much heartbreak and dread tied to our relationship and marriage that even the idea of talking to her made me anxious. At the time, I didn't fully understand why, and I brushed it off as normal emotions. But in reality, all of the traumatic experiences I had gone through back to back were piling up, weighing on me in ways I didn't recognize. I wasn't dealing with them properly—I was bottling everything up, burying it, and convincing myself that moving forward was enough.

That sinking feeling, that anxiousness, was the beginning of the anxiety that I deal with on multiple levels to this day. The depression that I thought had been at its worst in my teenage years had only grown worse over time because I had never truly processed it. Instead, I had tried to outrun it, but it had caught up to me.

I was reluctant to respond to her. Every instinct in me told me not to, but the truth was we were still married. There were things left unfinished—things we still had to address, whether I was emotionally ready for it or not. And no matter how much I told myself I was done, there was a part of me that still craved something I had never gotten from her: an apology.

I needed to hear her say she was sorry. I needed her to acknowledge what she had done. It was something I had never received before—at least not in a way that ever felt real. Every reconciliation before had been filled with excuses, reasons why it wasn't her fault, or ways to shift the blame. But never once had she genuinely taken accountability. And as much as I hated to admit it, part of me still held on to the hope that maybe this time would be different.

"Best I can be, you?" I finally responded.

It didn't take long before she found a way to begin playing on my emotions again. Through tears, she told me that regardless of what I had found, nothing had actually been going on. She insisted that if I had just talked to her, if I had just given her the chance to explain, everything would have been different.

I defended myself immediately. I did give her the opportunity. I had shown her the messages. I had confronted her head-on. But instead of explaining, she had shut down and gone cold.

She excused her reaction, saying she had just been caught off guard and didn't want to argue. But she admitted she never thought I would actually leave. She told me she had been completely blindsided when I left Florida, that she never saw it coming.

"I just wish you would have stayed, I wish you would've talked to me" she whispered. "I don't know what I'm supposed to do without you."

I took a deep breath and swallowed the lump in my throat. "I couldn't stay. You knew that." As much as it hurt, I told her again that I had meant what I said. Never again.

I waited for an apology.

It never came.

The conversation ran dry. And just like that, we hung up the phone.

After I hung up the phone, her words lingered in my mind. I knew I couldn't go back—going back was no longer an option. But hearing her cry still affected me, and she knew it would. As much as I wanted to stay firm in my decision, there was a part of me that wondered if I had overreacted, if I had left too quickly without giving her the chance to properly explain. But no matter how I tried to rationalize it, I knew the truth—flirting was still crossing the line, whether something further had happened or not. It was inexcusable, and that alone was enough for me to never even consider returning.

Still, it hurt. It hurt to feel like I had genuinely hurt her, even after all of the pain she had put me through. No matter how many times she had broken my heart, it didn't change the fact that I had once loved her with everything in me. That love hadn't just disappeared overnight, and it was unbearable to think of the kids too. I had grown so close to them over the course of our marriage, and even though I had long accepted that my wife's daughter wasn't biologically mine, we had built a father-daughter bond that was real. Walking away from them, from what I once knew as my family, was far more painful than I had initially allowed myself to admit.

But as much as it hurt, I knew I had made the right decision. No matter how much I cared, my wife's actions were inexcusable. She had crossed the line so many times before, and if I had gone back again, it would have never stopped. That thought had to be my anchor. I had to remind myself over and over again that this was for the best.

Still, there was another lingering truth that I couldn't shake —she wasn't the type to let go easily. The way she sounded on the phone, the way she framed the situation, made me believe that she wasn't looking to move toward divorce anytime soon. I knew that, despite everything, she would likely try to pull me back in, and the thought of that happening made my anxiety grow stronger. Because no matter how much she had hurt me, no matter how much logic told me to stay away, deep down inside... I knew I still loved her.

She kept the conversations light over the next week, carefully tiptoeing around any mention of our relationship. She stuck to topics she knew would grab my interest—things we had always enjoyed talking about. It started small, just occasional texts here and there, nothing serious, nothing emotional. I didn't even realize it at first, but I was growing fond of these casual interactions again. It felt comfortable, familiar, and before I knew it, I was sharing things with her too.

Then, she finally broke the ice. "I miss you."

I didn't even hesitate before responding. "I miss you too."

The words left my fingers almost instinctively, but the moment they were sent, I felt a pang of regret. I had spent so much time trying to convince myself I was moving forward, that I was strong enough to leave her in the past where she belonged. And yet, here I was, slipping right back into that same emotional pull she always seemed to have on me.

She didn't waste any time. She asked me to come back. This time, though, she wasn't just begging. There was more warmth, more explanation—more manipulation, though I didn't recognize it then. I told her the same thing I had told her before. That as much as I still loved her, as much as I still missed her, I no longer trusted her. I told her I had shifted my focus to my daughter, to rebuilding my life in Nashville, and that it was best for me to stay here and move forward.

That's when she hit me with something I wasn't expecting. "Well, I'm not filing for divorce, so we need to figure something out. If you want out of this marriage, you're going to have to file for it yourself."

I knew exactly why she said that. She knew I couldn't afford to file for divorce. And, more importantly, she knew I wasn't ready.

My wife had always known me better than I liked to admit, and she knew I had never been the one to end a relationship. Even when I knew things were over, I couldn't bring myself to be the one to make it final. She knew I still loved her, and she knew I wasn't strong enough to push the papers forward myself.

She had backed me into a corner, and I knew it.

I felt that sinking feeling in my stomach again, the one I had felt so many times before when I knew I was about to make the wrong decision. I knew exactly what was coming. It was only a matter of time before I gave in.

I hurried off the phone, telling her I had to go. I needed to think. I needed to let it sink in. But deep down, I already knew—we were likely headed towards getting back together. It wasn't a question of if, only a question of when. And I had no idea how to even begin processing that.

Our conversations increased over the next few weeks, each one becoming deeper and more centered around the idea of reconciliation. She was all in—she made it very clear that she wanted to get back together and fix our marriage. I, on the other hand, was extremely reluctant. I had my doubts, but at the same time, I knew I wasn't emotionally ready to completely let go. And the truth was, she knew it too.

Over time, I laid everything out on the table. I told her exactly what I expected moving forward, and I wasn't budging on any of it. If we were going to work on our marriage, it would have to be in Nashville. I wasn't leaving my daughter again, and I stood firm on that. My wife agreed to everything, making countless promises that my heart was eager to accept—but my mind was another story.

Once we had come to an agreement, we began searching for an apartment together. I let my sister know how much I appreciated all of her help and filled her in on my attempt at reconciliation. Bootsie had her reservations and understandably so, but she was supportive nevertheless and hopeful that things might finally work out the way I had always wanted them to.

We eventually settled on an apartment in Hermitage at Stewart's Ferry Apartments, a place I was already pretty familiar with. My cousin Ronnie and an old friend of mine had lived there before, and I had always liked the peaceful atmosphere. It had direct access to the greenway, with trails leading all the way to the dam or, if you went all the way in the other direction it led to downtown Nashville. It felt like a fresh start, or at least, I wanted to believe it was.

Before finalizing everything, I had a conversation with my daughter's mother. She was understandably concerned, and she made that very well known. She wasn't thrilled about the idea of my wife coming back into my life, but her biggest concern was that it might interfere with my growing relationship with our daughter. I reassured her that no matter what happened, my daughter remained my top priority. I wasn't going to let anything get in the way of that. Though hesitant, she agreed to do whatever she could to help things move forward peacefully.

The time finally came for me to sign the lease and move my belongings into the new apartment. Shortly after, my wife would work things out in Florida and eventually follow with the kids. That first day in our new home, we sat in the living room, surrounded by empty space and bare walls, talking about the future. It was good to see my wife in person again, especially when she was in this state of mind—hopeful, committed, and ready to make things work. There were still obvious concerns in the back of my mind, lingering doubts that wouldn't go away, but I did my best to push them aside.

We had to get it right this time. Not just for us, but for the kids. They were getting older, becoming more aware of their surroundings, and they deserved stability. They deserved to see love done right.

We needed to get it right—for them.

When my wife moved back, we held a lot of deep conversations face-to-face, and honestly, it started to feel more and more promising. She seemed like she had turned a curve, and she really seemed focused. Everything she had told me over the phone—the things I had my doubts about

—she was now actively trying to prove. She went out of her way to calm my doubts and get us into a healthy space. It genuinely felt like she was trying for our marriage.

She even went as far as burying the hatchet with my daughter's mother to help create a better relationship in her role as a stepmother. We even discussed and planned on doing the right thing by getting a paternity test for her daughter, so that we could finally put everything to rest and make the best decisions for everyone involved. Things started to line up, and they lined up fast. We settled into the apartment, worked on turning it into a home, and focused on building a future together.

The kids started school, where my wife's children attended alongside my daughter, and they became closer than ever. It was a bittersweet thing to witness—seeing them all together as siblings, growing up, bonding. For the first time in a long time, it felt like I could actually breathe. There were still doubts that lingered in the back of my mind because of everything we had been through, but this was the most promising our marriage had ever seemed. My wife really seemed like a different person, and for the first time, I let myself believe that maybe, just maybe, we could get this right.

Unfortunately, that feeling wouldn't last. After nearly a year of my wife being in Nashville, old problems resurfaced. The issue of getting a paternity test for her daughter continued to be a major divide between us. I wanted to do it because I felt it was the right thing to do—for everyone. My wife, on the other hand, still had her reservations and wasn't ready to take that step. What started as a quiet disagreement turned into tension, and that tension turned into arguments.

Eventually, the inevitable happened. She told me she was going back to Florida.

Unlike the separations in our past, this one didn't involve cheating. It wasn't some dramatic explosion or act of betrayal. But it was still heartbreaking. I had watched us build something, only to see it slip away again because we couldn't see eye to eye on a crucial issue.

But this time, I was different.

I stood firm on what I told her before she moved up to Nashville, and I didn't budge. There was no argument, no begging, no pleading. I told her if she wanted to leave, then she could go. And that was it. I would refocus my energy and attention back into my daughter and move forward without hesitation.

She didn't like my response, but I meant it. And just like that, almost as quickly as she had moved back, she was gone again.

The difference this time? I wasn't shattered.

I picked up the pieces quickly, and for the first time, I realized something—standing firm had built a strength inside of me I didn't even know was there. After everything, I wasn't broken this time. I was moving forward, and I wasn't looking back.

Adjusting to life on my own was tough, but this time it felt different. When my wife left, it wasn't just another separation—it was a complete shift in my reality. Initially, I had been excited about getting my own place, nervous about the idea of being on my own, but still ready to take that step. All of that had been derailed when my wife and I decided to get back together and get the apartment together. Now, instead of moving in alone and adjusting to independence, I was suddenly facing all of those emotions head-on, but now with the added weight of memories that came with sharing that space with someone who was no longer there.

The hardest part wasn't the loneliness—it was the memories. Every room held something that reminded me of my wife and the kids. The way the couch was arranged, the plates in the cabinets, even small things like a toy tucked into the corner of the living room would take me back to when we were a family. The nights were the hardest. I shed my fair share of tears, but this time, I didn't allow myself to drown in them like I had before.

I forced myself to move forward in ways I hadn't in the past. I started seeking out self-help content on YouTube, listening to other men's experiences with heartbreak, trauma, and toxic relationships. I reconnected with friends and family on a deeper level. Marriage has a way of pulling you away from those connections, and now I had the time and space to rebuild those relationships. I didn't isolate myself the way I had in the past—I made sure I was out and about, spending time with people who cared about me and wanted to see me do better.

I also threw myself back into physical fitness, knowing that it had helped me heal in the past. Running, lifting weights, and focusing on bettering myself physically helped me battle the emotions that still threatened to pull me back down. I also started making small changes to the apartment—rearranging furniture, adding new decorations, anything to change the space and make it feel more like my own instead of a reminder of what had been lost.

The World Cup was going on around this time, and it became an unexpected but welcome distraction. My childhood best friend, Julian, and I reconnected over the games, and it was refreshing to have something to look forward to that had nothing to do with my past relationship or my personal struggles. All of these small steps kept me occupied and, more importantly, kept me from reaching out to her. I had done that too many times before, and I knew where that road led.

but eventually, she would reach out to me again.

For months, we had no communication. I think she expected me to cave first, just like I had in the past. But this time, I didn't. I stayed focused on myself, on my daughter, and on rebuilding my life. When she finally did reach out, I wasn't surprised—it felt inevitable.

At first, the conversations were nothing serious. Just small talk like before. She'd ask how I was doing and test the waters to see if I would engage. I kept the conversations polite but distant. I had no intention of diving back into anything unless I knew for certain that things would be different.

But as time passed, I could tell something had shifted. I wasn't reacting the way I used to. I wasn't desperate for answers, I wasn't bitter or angry, and I wasn't going to entertain the same cycles. I stood firm in what I had told her before she left Nashville. If we were going to work on anything, it had to be under the right circumstances. I wasn't leaving Tennessee, my daughter was my first priority, and there would be no more games. I didn't say this with any anger or resentment—it was just the truth. And I think once she saw that I was serious, that I wasn't being cold but I also wasn't breaking, something changed for her.

There wasn't a big emotional plea, no grand gestures or deep conversations about our past this time. There was just a shift and slowly, she started talking about wanting to come back.

I had been through this cycle too many times, and I knew deep down that this wasn't healthy. But there was something about my wife that I still couldn't let go of, no matter how much I had healed or how strong I had become. The reality was, she had become my medication—she was the one thing that, no matter how much pain she had caused, still numbed the deeper pain I had never dealt with. The loss of Jenny, the trauma of 2009, all of it. My wife had become my addiction, and I wasn't ready to quit just yet.

And just like that, within a few months, she was back with me in Nashville—like she had never left.

When my wife moved back, there was an unspoken tension between us. We both knew that reconciling again wasn't going to be easy. The love was still there—at least, I believed it was—but the weight of our past, the betrayals, the back-

and-forth, all of it hung over us like a storm cloud waiting to burst. I genuinely wasn't sure if we were really capable of making it work.

Reconciliation is hard enough when it happens once. But when it becomes a cycle, it wears you down in ways you don't fully realize until you're in it again, staring at the same problems you swore you'd never face again. I knew that if I was going to give this another shot, something had to change. I had to change. I couldn't keep repeating the same patterns and expecting different results.

This time, I refused to be passive. In past reconciliations, I had taken a backseat, doing whatever it took to keep my wife happy, sacrificing my own needs and boundaries in the process. But this time, I set clear terms. I wasn't going to be a doormat anymore. I needed her to respect me, and if this was going to work, she had to understand that this was her final chance.

When the moment felt right, I had the conversation I had been holding back. I told my wife that if she left again, it wouldn't be up to her anymore—I would file for divorce myself. No more waiting, no more hoping she would do it if things fell apart again. I told her we needed to make up our minds once and for all, because the kids deserved stability. We had been so caught up in our own chaos that we had lost sight of what they needed—parents who weren't constantly playing this game of leaving and returning.

This time, she didn't argue. She agreed. She acknowledged that what we had been doing wasn't fair to anyone, especially the kids. She promised that this time, she was truly committed to making our marriage work. And surprisingly, she followed through.

Over the next few months, I saw a side of my wife I had never seen before. She put in the effort. She worked to rebuild trust. She was intentional about being present in our marriage and in our home. It was like I was meeting a different person, someone who had finally realized what was at stake. And for the first time in years, it felt like we weren't just trying to fix something broken—we were actually building something new.

Our relationship transformed in a way I never expected. We weren't just tolerating each other anymore; we were enjoying each other. I found myself looking at her differently, falling back in love with her in a way that was deeper than before. Seeing her be a mother to the kids, loving them, supporting them, being present—it changed something in me. This was the best period of our marriage, the most stable, the most fulfilling.

During this time, my wife began bringing up the idea of having another child—one that we planned for together. The kids would talk about wanting a little brother or sister, and she would remind me that this was something we had never experienced before. She believed that planning a child together, going through the journey of pregnancy with full intention and stability, would strengthen our bond and bring us closer than ever before.

At first, I was reluctant. As much as I wanted to believe in our progress, I couldn't ignore our history. A child wasn't something I wanted to bring into another unstable situation. But as the days passed, I caught myself thinking about it more and more, getting lost in the idea of finally experiencing something like that with my wife. Slowly, I started leaning toward wanting it, more than I was willing to admit at first.

Then one day, while I was at work, I felt my phone vibrate in my pocket. I stepped away from the line to check the message. It was from my wife—no words, just a picture.

A pregnancy test. Positive.

Whether I was ready or not, we were going to have our first child together.

CHAPTER 12

THE BEGINNING OF THE END

When my wife sent me the picture of the positive pregnancy test, a flood of emotions hit me all at once. The overwhelming feeling was excitement—real, genuine excitement. This was something we had talked about, something we had planned for. The idea that we were finally going to experience having a child together, from the very beginning, the right way, was something that brought a renewed sense of hope. I wanted to believe that this would be the fresh start our marriage needed, the missing piece that would strengthen our bond in ways we had never experienced before.

But behind the excitement, there were nerves—lingering, undeniable nerves. As much as I wanted to silence the doubt, the truth was, a small voice in the back of my mind wouldn't let me forget our past. I was tying myself to my wife permanently, no matter what. This child would always connect us, even if things didn't work out. And given our history, that thought carried weight. If she ever fell back into her old patterns, if she ever betrayed me again, how much worse would it be now that we had a child together?

I tried to shake the negativity, pushing it aside to focus on the positives. I reminded myself that this was a new chapter, and I needed to embrace it fully. No matter what had happened before, I made the decision to pour everything I had into my marriage and into this child. If this was going to work, I needed to be all in.

I promised myself that I would give her everything—every ounce of love and effort that I had. I would support her through every step of the pregnancy, making sure she never felt alone or unsupported. I told myself that if we failed, it wouldn't be because of me. I was going to be the best husband and father possible, no matter what. I had to believe that this time would be different.

So, I let go of my doubts. I chose to focus on the excitement, the possibilities, and the hope that maybe, just maybe, this would finally be the moment where everything truly changed for the better.

As time passed and my wife's belly began to grow, our relationship and marriage seemed to grow closer together as well. In fact, I don't think there was ever a time in our marriage where we felt more connected than during this period. Seeing my wife pregnant with our child created a love inside of me that I didn't even know existed. I had fallen in love with her before and had loved her more than I ever thought possible. But when she became pregnant with our child, something shifted. Seeing her body change, knowing that she was carrying our baby, deepened my love for her in a way I had never felt before. I cherished every moment of it.

The commitment I had made to be the best husband and father I could be felt effortless because it wasn't something I had to force—it came naturally. I was happy. I was eager to go to every appointment with her, to make every late-night Target run for whatever craving she had, to help prepare for our baby in any way I could. It felt like we were truly in this together, and I soaked up every moment.

As time went by, we started thinking about names, coming up with a short list depending on whether we were having a boy or a girl. I wanted a boy. I wanted a boy so badly. Of course, if we had a daughter, I would love her to the fullest—there was no question about that. I had always wanted a daughter with my wife, and I knew she would be an incredible mother to any child we had. But already having two daughters between us, the idea of a son excited me in a way that I couldn't explain. I imagined all the father-son things I never got to do with my own father. I wanted that experience, that bond, and I couldn't wait to find out if that was what we were going to have.

The day of our gender appointment finally arrived, and we were both anxious as we sat in the doctor's office. When the doctor looked at the ultrasound and told us we were having a healthy little boy, I almost fell out of my seat with excitement. A rush of emotions and thoughts flooded my mind—visions of playing ball with my son, teaching him things, watching him grow into his own person. In that moment, I swear I fell even further in love with her. This was everything I had dreamed of, and now, it was real.

We decided on his name. I had always loved this name we chose. We gave it an Italian twist that blended the name I liked with my wife's maiden name, a way to honor her father and carry on his family's name. Our son would be given four total names, just like me, with two middle names reflecting my wife's late uncle and my late mother, all tied together with an Italian influence and my last name.

And just like that, our son and first child together was on the way, and we couldn't have been more excited.

As my wife's pregnancy progressed, preparing for our son's arrival became the center of my world. It softened me as a husband but also ignited a fire within me that realigned my priorities in a way I had never experienced before. I became more focused, more driven, and more determined to make sure that when our son arrived, he was stepping into a world where his father had built a solid foundation for him.

Work became something I took more seriously than ever. I was no longer just showing up to earn a paycheck—I was striving for every possible promotion, every opportunity to better provide for our growing family. Beyond that, I made it a priority to be a better father to all of the kids, making sure they knew how much they were loved and cared for. I wanted to set an example for them, showing them what it meant to be a dedicated husband and father. I knew they were watching, absorbing everything, and I wanted them to see firsthand what it looked like for a man to truly step up for his family.

When I was home, I was all about my wife. I babied her throughout her pregnancy, doing everything I could to make her comfortable. My nights were spent rubbing her back or massaging her feet, talking with her about all the dreams we had for our son, and envisioning the future we were building together. My days off were spent shopping with her, preparing for the baby, and making sure we had everything our son could possibly need. It might have seemed exhausting from the outside looking in, but when you love someone the way I loved her, it never feels like work. Every moment with her, every little thing I could do to take care of her and our baby, felt natural.

And because of that, we grew closer than ever. We were finally feeling like we were on the right track, like everything we had been through had led us to this moment. For the first time in a long time, I truly believed we were getting it right. Maybe, just maybe, having a baby together was exactly what we needed to make our marriage everything we had always hoped it could be.

While everything was going wonderfully for me and my wife at this point in our marriage, especially throughout the pregnancy, there was an undeniable dark cloud hanging over me. My mom had grown sick leading up to my wife's pregnancy and was eventually diagnosed with cancer after my wife became pregnant. It was devastating to everyone, but especially to us because my mom was one of the most supportive people when it came to our marriage. She never gave up hope that we could work things out, and she wanted nothing more than to see us happy together.

My mom and I had an up-and-down relationship over the years, but as I got older, we grew closer. Her support throughout my marriage and for my wife only strengthened that bond. She understood the pain I had carried from losing Jenny and how it had completely shattered me. She saw firsthand how much I had loved Jenny, and she knew that her loss had left a hole in my life that I wasn't sure I'd ever be able to fill. I believe that's one of the main reasons she wanted so badly for things to work out with my wife—because she wanted me to have that kind of love again, something real, something lasting. She wanted me to be able to move forward, to have something positive to hold onto.

One of our last conversations is something that still sticks with me to this day. My mom told me that she really hoped that our baby would be a boy. She said she would love to be able to see and hold a little me again. The way she said it, the warmth in her voice—it was one of those moments that felt so full of hope, like she was hanging on to see that future. I think part of her truly believed that she would get to meet him, that she would have the chance to hold him in her arms and love him the way she had always loved me.

But that day never came.

My wife gave birth to a healthy little boy, a baby who looked just like me, just as my mom had imagined. But she wasn't there to see him. She wasn't there to hold him. And that thought still devastates me.

The grief was overwhelming. Losing my mom so close to the birth of my son felt like a cruel twist of fate, a painful reminder of how life gives and takes in equal measure. I tried my best to shift my focus back to my wife and our baby, but the weight of my mom's absence was heavy. I kept thinking about all the moments she would miss—the first time he opened his eyes, the first time he smiled, his first words, his first steps. I knew she would have loved him unconditionally, just as she had loved my daughter. I saw the love she had for my daughter firsthand, the way she cherished every moment with her, and it breaks my heart that my sons never got to experience that. They never got to meet their grandmother.

Her passing cast a shadow over what should have been one of the happiest moments of my life. There were times I felt guilty for being excited about my son's birth while also mourning the loss of my mother. There were nights I sat alone, holding my newborn son, staring at his tiny face and thinking about how much she would have adored him. I wished she could see him. I wished she could see me as a father and be there to guide me, to reassure me that I was doing a good job.

Despite the pain, I knew I had to keep moving forward. I had a wife and a newborn son who needed me. And in a way, I felt like carrying on, being the best father I could be, was a way of honoring my mother. She wanted me to have love in my life. She wanted me to be happy. So I held on to that. Even through the heartbreak, I did my best to focus on the future—on my wife, on our baby, on the life we were building.

But even now, I still think about what could have been. What it would have been like if she were still here, if she had gotten the chance to meet my son, to hold him, to love him the way I know she would have. And that, more than anything, is what I'll always carry with me.

As soon as our son was born, I was obsessed with him. I wanted to be involved in everything that had to do with him. I couldn't hold him enough. I couldn't hug him enough. I couldn't kiss him enough. No amount of love in the world felt like enough to give him. From the moment he was placed in my arms, it was like something inside me shifted permanently. He took to me almost immediately, always comfortable, always at ease. I could make him laugh so easily, and I absolutely loved it. I lived for his laughter. I would do the silliest things just to hear it, and every time I succeeded, it felt like the greatest accomplishment in the world.

Feeling this overwhelming love for my son and then seeing my wife care for him, nurture him, and love him the way she did—it only deepened my feelings for her. It strengthened the connection between us in a way I had never experienced before. I allowed myself to fall completely, as far as my heart would take me, and I loved every second of it. I loved her on a level that I didn't even know I was capable of. I found myself telling her this constantly, reminding her how much I loved her and how I was falling even deeper in love with her every day.

It was exciting. It felt like I was healing from the inside out, like everything in the past was finally washed away. Because of our son, we had a whole life ahead of us, full of promise. For the first time in a long time, I felt secure, stable, and at peace with where I was in life.

That feeling carried into every part of my life. There was a new pep in my step. I stood taller, walked with more confidence. I excelled at work, getting promoted twice. Life was good. It felt perfect, like we had finally made it. Like everything we had been through—all the struggles, all the heartbreak, all the second chances—had led us exactly where we needed to be.

Sometimes, I find myself thinking about that time in our lives, wishing we could have found a way to build off of that moment and keep that version of our marriage alive. It was one of the happiest times in my life. But it also serves as another harsh reminder of how quickly life can change.

After my wife gave birth to our son and things started settling back into a routine, the regular stresses of everyday life began creeping back into focus. During the pregnancy, we had been riding a wave of excitement and positive emotions, but now, reality was setting in. My wife's maternity leave was over, and I had to return to work, which meant the help I had been providing at home was suddenly cut in half. The long hours and financial strain began to take a toll, and even though I was determined to keep everything together, it was getting harder to ignore the weight of it all.

My wife had rarely worked throughout our marriage, primarily staying home to take care of the kids. I never had an issue with that, but with another mouth to feed, the pressure on me intensified. I was already working six days a week after being put on child support for my daughter, and the financial hit was significant. Most of my shifts stretched well over ten hours a day, and by the time I got home, I barely had a moment to catch my breath before gearing up to do it all over again the next day. My one day off was devoted to my daughter, but even that time was now split—my wife needed my help, the other kids needed attention, and I felt like I was being pulled in a hundred different directions.

I hadn't anticipated how difficult this transition would be, but I kept pushing forward, telling myself it was all part of being a father and a husband. The exhaustion was overwhelming, but I refused to complain. If keeping my family happy meant sacrificing my own peace, then so be it.

There were things about my wife's behavior that started to bother me as time passed, but I kept those thoughts to myself. I had spent so much time fighting for our marriage, for our family, that I wasn't about to let stress and exhaustion make me second-guess everything we had built. So, I did what I had always done—I bottled it up. I focused on being the best provider I could be, convinced that if I just kept my head down and kept going, things would eventually fall into place.

But looking back, I realize now that bottling everything up didn't make the problems go away. It only delayed the inevitable.

I found myself doing a pretty good job keeping it all together despite how I felt. I got quite addicted to energy drinks during that time, substituting sleep with 5-hour energy shots instead. Despite all the time constraints, there were still moments that my wife and I would find here and there to reel us back in romantically, but over time, those moments became less and less.

I would eventually get transferred multiple times to different job locations that needed help, and the stress of work was starting to bleed over into the stress of home life. I tried my best to keep it all in, but the little things that were beginning to aggravate me were piling on top of each other rapidly. I absolutely respected everything my wife had to do at home and her responsibilities of being a mother to our kids, but I began to feel as if I was pulling a lot more of the weight that should have been shared.

Six days a week, I was coming home late after 10- to 12-hour shifts, only to find laundry for a family of five piled up, wrinkled and needing to be put away, along with a sink full of dishes with dried food from breakfast still stacked high. It was exhausting. For weeks, I didn't say a word, chalking it up to her having a rough day or possibly dealing with something deeper emotionally or mentally. I knew she battled depression as well, but so did I. And regardless of how I felt mentally and emotionally, I still made sure to handle business, whether at work or at home.

I contemplated mentioning anything for weeks—the last thing I wanted to do was start a fight. That was until she told me, flat out, that I needed to do more.

I needed to do more?

What more could I do?

I was floored by the statement. Somehow, between working six days a week, long shifts every day, dedicating my one-off day to the family, and spending whatever time I had left cleaning up or helping with the baby, she still felt like I wasn't doing enough. This was the straw that broke the camel's back.

For the first time, I opened up completely about how I had been feeling, letting her know that I didn't think it was fair that I was coming home late at night and having to do the dishes and laundry before going to bed. I knew that taking care of kids was demanding and exhausting, but at the same time, I strongly felt like she could be doing more. I had discussed this in confidence with my sister, who had a child as well, and she agreed that my wife should absolutely be pulling more weight.

To me, it felt like I was genuinely the only one doing anything around the house outside of taking care of the kids full-time. I understood that people had bad days, but I had grown up around strong women my entire life, and I saw them do much more than what was being done.

This admission did not sit well with my wife at all. She looked at me, appalled, as if I had just said something unforgivable.

The problem was, I was worn thin, and I stood firm by what I said.

This argument clearly struck a chord with both of us. There was so much left to be said, but we both bowed out early, knowing full well how our fights had escalated in the past. But because the argument had been cut short, the tension between us only built. Even as time passed and we seemed to move on from it, underneath it all, it remained an unresolved problem—one that neither of us agreed on.

The unresolved tension started taking its toll on our marriage in more ways than one. Any slight disagreement we had always had the bigger issue looming underneath it. Even if we tried to avoid bringing it up, the problem never really went away—it was still there, unspoken, but ever-present. I decided to stop pushing the issue. I put my head down and focused on keeping the peace, putting everyone else's happiness ahead of my own.

I found a way to handle the situation more efficiently without addressing it directly. I stopped coming home disappointed when I saw what hadn't been done. Instead, I adjusted my expectations and assumed it would be that way. I started waking up earlier, making it a point to help more with the kids and knock out whatever chores needed to be done before I left for work. That way, when I got home late at night, there would be less left to do.

My wife had said she felt like I needed to do more, so I decided I would bend over backward to find a way to do it. It was easier for me to take on the extra weight than to risk another argument that could spiral into something worse.

Despite my efforts, I knew she could sense that I was still upset, even if I wasn't saying it. The tension between us remained, unspoken but lingering in the air. Because of this, it took a major toll on the romantic aspect of our relationship.

Any married couple knows that when intimacy starts to fade, other emotions begin to take over. Insecurities start creeping in. Jealousy finds its way into conversations where it doesn't belong. Doubt starts seeping through the cracks. And that's exactly what happened.

The lack of intimacy began to take a toll on me tremendously. If there was one thing that had always shined between me and my wife, it was our love life. That was undoubtedly one of the best aspects of our relationship and marriage. With this now being affected in a negative way, it was starting to play mind tricks on me, drawing out insecurities and jealousy that I was doing everything I could to suppress. All the times she had cheated before started creeping back into my mind, and I was running out of excuses to silence those thoughts. Nobody wants to have that conversation. Nobody wants to ask why, but it had to be brought up.

When I finally mustered up the courage to address the elephant in the room, I was blindsided—because she confronted me first.

"Are you cheating on me?"

Wait, what?

My wife just asked me if I was cheating on her. I couldn't believe it. But at the same time, I felt oddly relieved. It was a strange mix of emotions.

"Of course I'm not cheating on you. What in the world kind of question is that?" I asked, caught completely off guard.

She replied, saying she felt like I was being different, that I was acting distant around her, that I wasn't showing affection the way I used to. At first, I dismissed it as nonsense—I had been making it a point to be my best around her and the kids. But then I thought about it more. Maybe, despite my efforts, the weight of how I truly felt was showing through more than I realized. Either way, I knew I wasn't cheating on her, and I expressed that as clearly as I could.

But with the conversation already out in the open, I took the opportunity to bring up what had been eating away at me as well. I told her how I had been feeling, how the lack of intimacy had been making me question things, how my mind kept dragging me back to all the times she had betrayed me before.

To my surprise, she actually took it lightly. In fact, we ended up laughing about it together a little. Maybe we were both just under too much stress, both too focused on adjusting to this new life we were building to recognize that we had been slipping away from each other. Whatever the case, the conversation seemed to ease the tension. We found our way back to each other, and our love life started to pick up again.

Things were getting better.

Then, just as we seemed to be falling back into place, I felt my phone vibrate in my pocket at work. I glanced at the screen.

One unread text message from my wife.

"I'm late. Can you please stop by the store and grab a pregnancy test on your way home?"

I stared at the message for a moment.

You have to be kidding me, I thought to myself.

That message completely caught me off guard. When I read it, I couldn't say that there wasn't any excitement, but it was completely overshadowed by concern. Our son was only one, and we were already struggling to navigate life after him. Neither one of us was truly ready for another baby—I knew it, and deep down, my wife knew it too. The thought of adding another child into the mix stirred a level of stress inside me that I wasn't sure we could handle.

Still, in the back of my mind, I reminded myself that it wasn't a positive test yet. She was late, but she had been late before. This didn't mean anything definitive. My wife shared that same sentiment, texting me throughout the night.

"I seriously hope I'm not pregnant. We're not ready for another baby yet," she messaged.

"It's okay. Don't worry," I replied. "You've been late before. This doesn't mean anything yet, so don't let yourself get worked up until you know for sure."

On my way home, I stopped by the store and picked up the most accurate pregnancy test they had available. I didn't rush—I drove home slowly, letting the weight of the possibility settle in. When I walked through the door, I handed my wife the bag. She took a deep breath, thanked me, and disappeared into the bathroom.

I waited anxiously, pacing the floor, telling myself it was going to be negative. That it had to be.

Then the bathroom door opened.

Her expression said it all. There was no excitement in her face, no relief. Only tears welling in her eyes.

"It's positive," she said, her voice cracking.

I exhaled slowly, unsure of what to say. "Oh wow, babe... I'm sorry."

She stepped toward me, her emotions breaking through as she wrapped her arms around me and started to cry. "What are we going to do?" she asked through her tears.

I pulled back slightly, cupping her face in my hands, making her look at me. "It might be difficult, and it might be unexpected, but no matter what, we are going to love this baby and give this baby the best life possible. We'll adjust. We'll figure it out."

I wiped her tears and kissed her forehead, holding her close for a few more moments, feeling the weight of what was happening press down on me.

And as I held her, I silently prayed that what I had just told her was true.

This unexpected pregnancy brought a wave of emotions that neither of us were fully prepared for. Initially, the stress hit hard. There were so many "what ifs" and uncertainties that filled our conversations, and the overwhelming reality of our situation loomed over us. But even in the midst of that chaos, something familiar started to happen—we were gradually being drawn closer together, just as we had during my wife's pregnancy with our first son.

I made it a point to constantly remind my wife that she wasn't in this alone. We were going to figure this out together, just like we always had. No matter how difficult things had been before, we had always managed to find a way through, and this would be no different. I knew she needed that reassurance, and truthfully, so did I.

Despite my efforts to stay positive, there was no denying that this pregnancy came with a new set of challenges. Our apartment was already feeling tight, and adding another baby into the mix would make it nearly impossible to stay there long-term. Financially, things weren't in the best place either. Even though I had been promoted twice, my wife being out of work and now expecting again meant our expenses were only going to increase. It was a lot to take in, and we knew we had a limited amount of time to figure everything out.

Nine months. That was all we had to prepare for another life-changing moment. And ready or not, it was coming.

I immediately started looking for opportunities to increase my income. I had already cut back from working six days a week after our first son was born to be more present at home, but now, with another baby on the way, I had no choice but to take on more hours again. I spoke with my boss, and he offered me the option to work six days a week for as long as I needed. There was a catch, though—those extra shifts wouldn't always be at my regular store. I'd be moved around to different locations that needed coverage, which meant an inconsistent routine and even more exhaustion.

I talked it over with my wife, and we both agreed that it was the best option we had. I wasn't happy about it, but I knew I had to do whatever it took to make sure our growing family was provided for. Work had already been stressful with management changes and constant turnover, but knowing that the extra effort was contributing to a greater goal helped me push through.

The next challenge was finding a bigger place. Our apartment was no longer enough, and we both knew it. With another baby coming, we needed a house—something neither of us had ever tried to get before. We had no clue where to start.

We spent hours researching, reaching out to different lenders, and working with a real estate agent who connected us to different programs we might qualify for. We toured homes, hoping that one would be ours, but every time we thought we found the right one, reality hit us hard. My income alone wasn't enough to qualify, and without a second income from my wife, every door kept closing in our faces.

It was a gut punch. The excitement we had felt about moving into a house turned into disappointment as rejection after rejection came our way. I didn't say it out loud, but deep down, it frustrated me that I was carrying all the financial weight while my wife was still at home. I understood that she was raising the kids, but that didn't make it any easier to accept that we weren't where we needed to be because I simply couldn't do it all on my own. Still, I kept my frustration to myself. There was no point in adding another fight to the pile when we already had so much on our plates.

Just when it felt like we were running out of options, something unexpected happened. We came across a listing for a single-family home for rent in Murfreesboro. It wasn't the house we had dreamed of buying, but it was exactly what we needed—a home big enough for our family, in a good location, and within our budget.

We called the owners, explained our situation, and for the first time in months, we weren't met with a rejection. Instead, they listened. They understood. They were willing to work with us. Within days, we had signed the lease. After months of stress and feeling like we were stuck, we finally had a home.

The weight that had been pressing down on us suddenly felt lighter. It wasn't just about the house—it was about what it represented. For the first time in a long time, it felt like things were finally falling into place.

While we were celebrating the move, there was another battle I was fighting—one that took a toll on me in ways I didn't fully understand at the time.

My relationship with my daughter was becoming more strained by the day. My daughter's mother and my wife had never had the best relationship, and what had once been a tense coexistence had now turned into something much worse. The positive progress I had made with my daughter was now unraveling, and I found myself in and out of court trying to fight for more time with her.

The stress of the legal battles, combined with everything else going on, pushed me to my breaking point. It felt like I was being pulled in every direction, trying to be the best husband, the best father, the best provider, but no matter what I did, I felt like I was falling short somewhere.

I hated the way things were playing out with my daughter's. I hated that my time with her was being affected by problems that weren't between us but between the adults around her. And I knew that as much as I was trying to balance everything, I was losing precious time with her—time that I would never get back.

Even though my wife and I had finally secured a home for our growing family, there was an undeniable pain in knowing that another part of my family was slipping further and further away. I couldn't help but wonder if, in trying to build something stable for one part of my life, I was unintentionally losing another.

Through all of this, there was one thing I held onto—faith. As difficult as it was, I knew that God had brought us this far, and He wouldn't fail us now. We had a home, we had each other, and soon, we would have another beautiful baby boy. Even with all the struggles, I had to believe that we were on the right path.

And now, with our house finally secured, all that was left to do was prepare for the arrival of our newest son.

As my wife's pregnancy progressed and the final months approached, my focus was split between preparing for our newest son's arrival and navigating a heartbreaking decision regarding my daughter.

Court with my daughter's mother had been ongoing for months, leading nowhere productive for either of us. My wife and I were preparing to move to Murfreesboro with the kids, transitioning everyone to a new school, while my daughter's mother had been making plans of her own—plans that completely caught me off guard.

She informed me that she and her boyfriend were looking to relocate, not just to a different part of Tennessee but completely out of state. My visitation with my daughter's had already been limited due to court, and now I was faced with the impossible decision of either giving my blessing for her to move or fighting it in court—a battle I simply didn't have the resources to fight anymore. I had exhausted everything. I was completely drained, financially and emotionally.

Had I had the means, I would have continued fighting. But I had no other option. And if giving my consent meant some kind of peace, then so be it.

My daughter's mother assured me that if I agreed, she would drop the court battle and instead encourage a better relationship between me and my daughter. She promised ongoing communication, shared photos and videos, and visits whenever possible.

I didn't believe her.

But I also knew I had no other option. And as much as I hated it, part of me did crave peace after months of relentless stress and conflict. So I agreed. My daughter and her mother were gone, just like that.

It was the deepest kind of pain. I felt like I had sacrificed my relationship with my daughter for the sake of peace, even though the reality was I simply didn't have the means to continue the legal fight.

Losing that battle as a father left me broken in a way I still struggle to put into words.

But I did what I always did—I bottled it up and shifted my focus back to my family and our move.

My wife and I spent the final months of her pregnancy preparing for our transition into our new home in Murfreesboro. The house would give us the space we desperately needed, including an extra bedroom and a fenced-in backyard for the kids to play in. It was something we had never had before—our own house, a house we could finally call more than just a temporary home.

It felt like we were moving in the right direction.

Our youngest son was born in January of 2017, a healthy, beautiful baby boy. As much as we were excited and overjoyed, the absence of my daughter in that moment hit me hard. She had been there for our first son's birth, but this time, she was nowhere near. The reality of that cut deep, but I tried to push it aside and focus on the happiness of the moment.

Despite all the stress leading up to it, our newest son's arrival brought a renewed sense of optimism. My wife seemed more energetic, more excited about life. We even took a family trip to New York to visit her dad's side of the family. It was my first time visiting New York City, and I loved every bit of it. The kids had a blast, and for me, that trip made me feel closer to my wife than ever. It felt like we needed that trip. We needed that win after everything we had been through.

By mid-July, we officially moved into our new home in Murfreesboro. We had saved money from our tax returns to help with the move and furnish the house. It was an accomplishment—one that had taken everything we had to make happen. But finally, we could breathe. The chaos was over. Our baby boy was here. We were in our new home, the one we had spent months fighting for. We had done it. Together.

For any other married couple, this should have been the defining moment—the one where they looked at each other and knew there was no turning back, no more doubts, no more thoughts of leaving. We had fought side by side for so long, and we had won.

That's what this moment did for me. It further solidified my love for my wife, bringing our relationship to a whole new level. I had no doubts left in my mind. Walking away from each other at this point wasn't even a thought anymore. How could it be after everything we had just survived together?

But I had no idea just how wrong I was.

CHAPTER 13

THE FINAL BETRAYAL

A few months after our youngest son was born, my wife started becoming more and more distant. Her behavior was starting to resemble the patterns I had seen before, the same ones that had led to our past separations. I tried to ignore it at first, convincing myself that maybe I was just being paranoid. But deep down, I knew better. I had lived through this cycle too many times before not to recognize what was happening.

My wife's decision-making became more independent—almost as if she didn't feel the need to consult me about anything anymore. She was doing things on her own, stressing how much she wanted personal space, and disregarding my opinions entirely. The pit in my stomach grew heavier with each passing day, that all-too-familiar feeling creeping back in, warning me that something was wrong.

Then, out of nowhere, she told me she wanted to take a trip down to Florida to visit her mom—but she wanted to go alone. She said she needed space and time to herself, but she wanted to take the kids.

The moment she said it, my gut twisted into knots. I had been here before. I had seen this script play out in our marriage before. I knew what it meant, even if I didn't have solid proof yet.

At first, I tried to be understanding. I didn't want to spark an argument, so I reluctantly agreed. Maybe I was overreacting, I told myself. Maybe I was letting past trauma dictate my response. Maybe, just maybe, this was actually about her needing a break and not something worse.

But when she left, her communication with me became scarce. She barely answered my texts or calls. When she did respond, her replies were brief, generic—completely devoid of warmth or any indication that she missed me or our home.

I knew.

I knew something was happening, but I didn't know what.

At first, she had planned to stay for a week. But then a week turned into two. And the longer she stayed, the more disconnected she became.

I confronted her over the phone, pressing her for answers. "Just tell me the truth. What's going on?"

"Nothing," she said. "I just need more time here."

"More time for what? What aren't you telling me?"

"Nothing is going on. You're overthinking again."

It was the same deflection, the same gaslighting, the same manipulation I had endured before. It made my blood boil. I knew she was lying, but she refused to give me anything.

At that point, I stopped pushing. If she wasn't going to tell me, I wasn't going to beg. I forced myself to refocus, shifting my energy toward what I could control—taking care of our home, looking after the responsibilities she had left behind. But in the back of my mind, I braced myself for the inevitable.

And then it came.

She finally returned home, but she was even more distant than before. Her coldness was undeniable. She acted like she didn't even want to be in the same room as me, brushing past me like a stranger.

For weeks, I held my tongue. I gave her space. I waited. But then one day, she finally broke the silence.

"We need to talk," she said, standing in the doorway of our bedroom.

The moment those words left her mouth, my stomach dropped.

Here it was.

I knew what was coming, but that didn't stop my heart from racing. I followed her outside to the back patio, preparing myself for whatever she was about to say.

"I want a divorce," she said.

What?

I blinked, completely caught off guard. "What?"

"I want a divorce," she repeated, her tone emotionless.

I stared at her, my mind racing to process what I had just heard. My whole body went numb.

"You're kidding, right?" I finally said, forcing a dry laugh.

"I'm serious."

She didn't hesitate. She didn't stutter. She didn't even flinch.

It was clear now. She had planned this.

The trip to Florida, her distance, her coldness—it had all been leading up to this. She had spent weeks preparing for this moment, setting herself up for this decision while keeping me completely in the dark.

I felt like a fool.

All the work I had put into our marriage, all the sacrifices, all the forgiveness—I had done everything in my power to make this work, and now, she was the one walking away?

The anger inside of me started to rise. How could she do this? After everything?

She sat there calmly, like she had already mapped out exactly how this conversation was going to go. Like she had rehearsed it. Every time I spoke, she had a pre-planned reply, completely void of any emotion.

I noticed the way she dismissed the kids when they tried to come into the room, shooing them away like this was just a casual discussion, as if we were just deciding what to cook for dinner.

She didn't care.

She didn't care what happened to me next. She had already figured out her next move.

I sat there in stunned silence, the weight of everything hitting me all at once.

All I could think about was our sons.

We had fought so hard to create a life for them. We had built a home, started a family. And now, with a single conversation, she was throwing it all away.

She wasn't just ending our marriage—she was stealing something away from our children. She was taking away the life I had fought so hard to build for them, robbing them of the chance to grow up with both of their parents in the same home.

I felt sick.

This was it.

Everything I had feared, everything I had tried to prevent—it was all crashing down right in front of me, and there was nothing I could do to stop it.

I was immediately sent into fight-or-flight mode emotionally. My mind flooded with memories—our years together, the struggles we had endured, the dreams we had built, all turning to ash in an instant. And as I sat there in stunned silence, looking at my wife, I realized something that shook me to my core.

She didn't care.

There was no remorse in her eyes. No hesitation in her voice. No flicker of the love we had once shared. It was as if this conversation was nothing more than an item on a checklist—something she had planned, prepared for, and now was simply executing.

What was her goal in all of this?

I said the only thing I could bring myself to say.

"Fine. If that's what you want, then leave. You want this? Go. Because I'm not leaving. I'm not leaving those kids, and you're not taking them away from me."

She chuckled.

I felt my blood boil. Was she serious right now? She had just obliterated everything I had worked for, everything we had fought for, with one word—and now she was laughing?

A sick feeling twisted in my gut.

"You need to go. Now. You need to leave. Get out of my house," I said, my voice rising.

"You need to go before I call the cops," she said, calm as ever.

I stared at her in disbelief. "Are you serious? My name is on this lease, yours isn't. I literally pay for everything here. This is my house," I said, my voice shaking with anger. "You want this, you go."

"I'm calling the cops," she replied flatly.

"Fine, call them," I shot back. "Let's see what they say. I'm not going anywhere."

And then, she did it.

She dialed 911, put the phone on speaker, and with a steady, calculated voice, she spoke.

"Hello? Yes. I'm calling because I just told my soon-to-be ex-husband that I want a divorce, and he's getting irate and trying to force me to leave. But we have multiple kids here, and I fear for my safety. Can you please send an officer out?"

I sat there in complete disbelief, listening to her blatantly lie with no hesitation, no remorse.

That was the moment I knew.

I had questioned it before, I had ignored the signs, I had excused and justified so much—but now? After watching her do what she just did?

There was something seriously wrong with her. And it went far deeper than I had ever imagined.

The silence between us was suffocating as we waited for the cops to arrive. I kept my distance from her, refusing to engage in whatever game she was trying to play. After hearing her blatantly lie to the dispatcher, any remaining trust I had in her was completely gone.

When the officers finally knocked on the door, I greeted them and led them into the dining room. They listened as I explained everything, sticking to the truth about our disagreement—not denying that it was serious, but making it clear that there was no yelling, no threats, no aggression. My wife, however, doubled down on her fabricated story, telling them she felt unsafe and needed me to leave.

I couldn't believe what I was hearing. The woman I had fought for, forgiven, and loved through everything was now standing in front of me, twisting reality in her favor without a shred of guilt. She knew what she was doing. She knew what she wanted, and she had planned it all in advance.

The cops tried to stay neutral, but I could already tell where this was heading. "One of you needs to leave," one of them said.

I looked at her. "Then she should go," I said firmly.

She scoffed and shook her head. "No, he should leave," she shot back.

I held my ground, explaining that this was my home, my name was the only one on the lease, and I was the sole provider for the household. She argued that she was the mother of the children and that she needed to stay.

The cops sided with her.

I felt my blood boil. I knew how these situations played out. It didn't matter that I was the one being wronged, that I was the one who had been betrayed. The reality was simple—the man is guilty until proven innocent, and the woman is innocent until proven guilty.

"You need to leave, just for the night," the officer said, almost sympathetically.

I clenched my jaw and shook my head. "No."

My wife looked shocked, and so did the officers.

"I'm not leaving my home because of something she started. This isn't right, and it's not okay. If the roles were reversed, you'd be telling me the same thing. I pay for everything here. I work my butt off to provide for this family, and now, just because she says she wants a divorce, I'm supposed to leave? No. I won't."

The cops stared at me for a moment before one of them sighed. "Well, someone needs to leave, because we can't walk away from this unresolved."

I took a deep breath, forcing myself to stay calm. "There is no problem on my end. I'll sleep on the couch. I'll stay out of her way. If you have to come back out, I'll leave. But I'm not walking out of my house for no reason."

The officers exchanged glances before turning to her. "Are you okay with that?" one of them asked.

She crossed her arms. "No, but if I don't have a choice, then whatever. I'll just stay in the room."

They warned us both that if they had to return, someone would absolutely be leaving in handcuffs. Then, they left.

She was furious, but I didn't care. If she wanted out of this marriage, she could go. I wasn't the one who had broken it.

I set up on the couch and prepared to go to sleep, but she had other plans. Hours passed before she finally emerged from the bedroom, dressed to perfection. Her hair, makeup, and outfit were carefully put together—far more effort than she ever made just to run errands. She was going out, and she wanted me to know it.

I didn't say a word. I saw her. I acknowledged it. But I didn't give her the satisfaction of a reaction.

She left, and I spent the night with the kids, tucking them in and making sure they were okay. When they were asleep, I laid back on the couch, staring at the ceiling, shaking my head. What has my life become?

Shortly after dozing off, I heard the front door open. I sat up, peeking around the corner to see her quietly slipping in.

She was barefoot, holding her heels in one hand and a takeout box in the other. She walked straight past me without a word, disappearing into the bedroom and shutting the door behind her.

I laid back down, shutting my eyes, willing myself to sleep.

I had no idea that the next morning would change my life forever.

The next morning, I woke up to the sound of my wife moving around the house, making noise from room to room. I glanced at the clock—it was barely past 5:00 a.m. Still groggy, I got up to use the bathroom, and when I came out, I noticed her getting the boys dressed.

I rubbed my eyes, trying to wake up. "Why are you getting the boys dressed at 5:00 in the morning? It's summer. Where are you going this early?" I asked.

"To the park," she said nonchalantly.

I narrowed my eyes. "To the park? At 5:00 a.m.? That makes no sense. Why so early?"

"I want to start my day early and just take the boys to the park. Is that okay?" she snapped.

Something felt off, but I didn't have the energy to argue. "Whatever floats your boat, I guess."

I made my way to the kitchen, started a pot of coffee, and decided to keep my thoughts to myself. The last thing I wanted was another argument. She finished getting the boys ready, and I walked over to kiss them goodbye, telling them to have a good time. She barely acknowledged me as she grabbed the diaper bag and walked out the door.

I stood by the kitchen window, sipping my coffee as I watched them back out of the driveway. Me and my dad had just replaced the front end parts to her van with brand-new ones, and I was glad to see it was running smoothly again. As she drove down the street, I was just about to turn away from the window when something caught my eye—another vehicle pulling into the driveway.

I squinted. A sheriff's vehicle.

Then another.

My stomach dropped.

Two officers exited the vehicles and headed straight for the back door—They had just left out of that door minutes ago.

Boom. Boom. Boom.

They banged on the door hard, and my heart started pounding in my chest.

What in the world is going on?

I opened the door quickly. "Can I help you, gentlemen?"

One of the officers, standing firm, asked, "Are you Joseph Norfleet?"

"Yes, that's me. Is there something wrong?"

"Mr. Norfleet, have you ever heard of an order of protection?"

I blinked in confusion. "I'm aware of what that is, but why do you ask?"

The officer pulled out a thick stack of papers. "Mr. Norfleet, this is an ex parte order of protection filed by your wife. You have fifteen minutes to collect anything of importance and exit the house promptly."

I felt like the ground had been ripped from beneath me.

"Are you kidding me?" I scoffed, shaking my head. "I didn't even do anything! How in the world could she get an order of protection and force me to leave my own home?"

The officer didn't flinch. "That's up to the judge to decide. We're just giving the orders now. Please, sir, you have fifteen minutes. Gather your belongings quickly and exit the premises. You are not allowed back at the property, and if you are seen at the property or come anywhere near your wife or your children, you will be arrested."

My stomach twisted at his words. "My sons too?"

I couldn't even process what was happening, but I knew I had no time to argue. If I didn't move fast, I might end up losing even more than I already had. Rushing through the house, I grabbed a garbage bag and started throwing in clothes, work uniforms, and any essentials I could find. My hands were shaking as I packed, my mind racing for some logical explanation.

What did she say? What did she do? How did this happen?

After about ten minutes, I walked out of the house, garbage bag slung over my shoulder like some stranger being evicted from his own life. The officers stood by, watching me closely as I walked to my car.

I turned back to them, still desperate for answers. "Do you have any details whatsoever? Some kind of explanation? This makes no sense to me."

One officer simply handed me the paperwork. "Everything you need to know should be in that order. Just sign here and be on your way."

I numbly took the pen and signed, knowing I had no other choice.

As I pulled out of the driveway, I watched in my rearview mirror as the officers drove away in the opposite direction, leaving me behind with nothing but a garbage bag of clothes and absolutely no idea where to go.

Clearly rattled by what had just happened, I decided not to drive any further and pulled over so I could think. I needed to wrap my mind around everything that had just gone down that morning. It was still early, and I was supposed to be working that day, but there was no way I could function like this. I grabbed my phone and called my boss.

"Hey, I'm sorry to call you out of the blue like this with such heavy news, but I'm not going to be able to make it in today," I told him, trying to steady my voice.

My boss had known me for years and was familiar with the ups and downs of my marriage. He didn't even sound surprised when I explained the situation. "I get it," he said. "Take whatever time you need and get things sorted. Just keep me posted."

That was a huge relief. One less thing to worry about. But as soon as I hung up the phone, the weight of it all came crashing down on me again.

I had nowhere to go.

I tried to convince myself that I had been here before, that I could handle this, but this time was different. My mom was gone, and my sisters weren't viable options. I didn't have many places to turn. That's when I thought of my dad.

I hesitated before calling. I had a good relationship with my dad, but we weren't particularly close. I had never leaned on him for something like this before. But at that moment, I didn't have any other options.

When he picked up, I took a deep breath.

"Hey, Dad, I'm sorry to call you out of the blue like this with such a heavy reason, but my wife just sprung on me that she wanted a divorce. It led to a disagreement, and now she's filed for an order of protection against me. I didn't do anything at all, and I have no idea how she managed to do that, but I can't go home, and I can't be around her or the kids. I don't know what to do, and I have no idea where to go."

There was a pause on the other end. My dad was quiet for a moment, processing everything I had just unloaded on him.

"Where are you right now?" he finally asked.

"I pulled over. I didn't know which direction to drive."

"Well, just stay right there," he said. "I'm leaving now, and I'll meet you there."

We hung up, and as I sat there waiting for him, the adrenaline started to wear off. The built-up anger settled down with it, and sadness began to set in. The reality of what was happening hit me like a freight train.

It was one thing to be away from my wife, but being completely cut off from my kids? That was excruciating.

I couldn't call. I couldn't text. I had no way of knowing if they were okay. That kind of powerlessness creates a sense of urgency and angst that just won't settle. It was a horrible, helpless feeling, and the more I thought about it, the worse I felt.

By the time my dad pulled up, I was sitting in my car with tears in my eyes. He got out and walked over to me.

"How are you holding up?" he asked, his voice filled with concern.

I shook my head. "As best as I can be right now. This hurts, man."

Without hesitation, he reached in and hugged me.

"You don't have to worry about a roof over your head," he reassured me. "Come on, follow me home."

And just like that, I had somewhere to go. But the battle was far from over.

CHAPTER 14

GAME OVER

When I first got to my dad's house, I felt an immediate sense of relief—at least for the moment. I had a roof over my head, a place to go, and someone who was willing to help me get back on my feet. But as the hours turned into days, the reality of everything started to set in, and the weight of it all became almost unbearable.

Here I was again, having to start over. Having to press the reset button after years of effort, hard work, and growth. Everything I had fought for—my home, my family, my marriage—was now slipping through my fingers, and there was nothing I could do about it. The devastation hit in waves, and this time, it felt even worse than before because I wasn't just a man losing his wife. I was a father, now separated from all three of my children with no contact and no control over the situation.

God bless my dad, because I know how hard he tried to make things comfortable for me, even though I wasn't the greatest company in those first few days. I was grateful for his help, but I struggled to show it. I was stuck in my own head, trying to rationalize everything that had happened, searching for any way to make sense of it all.

It was confusing because nothing about this felt real. My mind kept bouncing between different outcomes, playing out possibilities of what might happen next. A court date was looming, and depending on what the judge decided, this situation could go in multiple different directions. The uncertainty was overwhelming.

And yet, deep down, something inside me told me this wasn't permanent. I don't know if it was denial, hope, or just sheer instinct, but something in the back of my mind kept whispering that this was temporary. Maybe that was just me holding on to the last shred of optimism I had left. Maybe I just wasn't ready to accept the truth yet.

Despite how I was feeling, I knew I needed to get my priorities in line. The court date was coming whether I was ready or not, and I had to be prepared. There was no other option. This wasn't just about me—this was about my kids. They needed me in their lives, and with their mother making the decisions she was, they needed me now more than ever. With that thought in mind, I started shifting my focus, making every move I made from that point forward about my children.

The first thing I needed to do was get my finances in order. I knew I didn't have enough to hire an attorney, and with the restraining order forcing me to continue paying for a home I no longer resided in, as well as all the utilities, I had very little to work with. I called my boss at work and told him to give me as many hours as possible, to send me anywhere he needed me to go, and he agreed. That helped maximize my main income, but I knew it still wouldn't be enough—I needed more.

I started researching different ways to make extra money and cutting back on any unnecessary expenses. I looked at my phone bill and realized my wife was still on my plan. That was an easy decision—I called Verizon and had her removed. While I was at it, I switched to a cheaper plan and even upgraded my phone, saving money in the process. Next was the internet. It wasn't a necessity, and I had been the one paying for it the whole time. The kids had plenty of other things to do, and the only one who would benefit from it now was her. That was another bill I cut. I even shopped around for better car insurance, eliminating anything that wasn't essential. Every dollar I saved was another step toward stability, and cutting her off financially was an added bonus.

While focusing on my finances, I also began settling into the vacant room at my dad's house. It was blank and lifeless, previously belonging to my stepsister before she moved out. My dad had put a twin bed and a dresser in there, and while it wasn't much, it was going to be home for now. I unpacked my clothes from the trash bag I had carried out of the house and put them in the closet and dresser. I debated setting up the room to make it more comfortable, but every time I thought about it, my emotions got the best of me. Something about decorating the room felt like admitting that I was staying, like I was settling into a new life that I wasn't ready to accept yet. Instead, I spent most of my time downstairs watching TV, trying to keep my mind occupied.

Living with my dad took some adjusting for both of us. He was used to living alone, and I was used to being a family man. Our realities had collided unexpectedly, and while we clashed here and there, he truly stepped up to the plate when I needed him most. This time in my life brought us closer than we had ever been before, creating a bond that was long overdue, and I'll always be grateful for that.

Just as I was getting things in order, another hit came my way—one I hadn't anticipated. My wife's stepfather called. I missed the call at first, but when I listened to the voicemail, my stomach dropped. He was calling to inform me that I needed to return the car I had been driving. Since my name wasn't on the title and his still was, I could either buy it outright or give it back. He apologized for the inconvenience but said those were my only two options.

I sat there, completely blindsided. The car situation had always been complicated. I had my own vehicle throughout our marriage, but one Christmas Eve, a woman high on pills had darted out in front of me, totaling my car. After receiving the insurance payout, I used the money to buy my wife a new van, taking her car in return. But that car was technically still owned by her stepfather. The only car with my name on it was the van she was driving.

I had no idea what I was going to do. I didn't have the money to buy another car, and even though she didn't deserve anything from me, I refused to take the van away from her. I wasn't going to do anything that would negatively affect the kids. So, with no other choice, I agreed to return the car.

When her stepfather came to pick it up, I found my way to the room, shut the door, and sat on the bed, overwhelmed. This was yet another problem that I had no answer for. Full of frustration, anger, and heartbreak, I buried my face in my hands, doing everything I could to keep from breaking down completely. I tried to cry as silently as possible—I didn't want my dad to hear.

A little while later, he knocked on my door. I wiped my face, opened the door, and he stepped inside. Without saying anything, he hugged me.

"I hate to see you like this," he said. "But I don't want you stressing over something that's going to work itself out. You'll get through this."

I nodded, appreciating his words but still feeling lost. That night, I prayed. I prayed harder than I had in a long time. I prayed for guidance, for strength, for an answer. At some point in the middle of my prayer, I fell asleep, exhausted in every possible way.

The next morning, my dad knocked on the door again. I got up and let him in, and he sat down on the edge of the bed.

"I've been thinking a lot about your situation," he said. "And I hate seeing you stuck like this. I know you've been doing everything you can to get back on your feet, and I want to help you."

I looked at him, confused. "What do you mean?"

He smiled. "You know my truck? I know it's not brand new, but I've had that thing for years, and I know every inch of it inside and out. I know it runs great, and I know it's reliable. I've been finishing up rebuilding the Dodge, so I want you to have it."

I stared at him, stunned. "You're serious?"

He nodded. "I've never been able to give you anything like this before, and I want to do this for you. You deserve it."

I couldn't believe what I was hearing. My dad was giving me his truck—just like that. Not only was he solving one of the biggest problems I had no answer for, but he was giving me something in better condition than any vehicle I had ever owned.

I didn't know what to say. All I could do was hug him and cry.

Receiving the truck from my dad changed everything for the better. I don't think he fully realizes how much he actually helped me moving forward. That truck wasn't just a vehicle—it was a lifeline, a symbol that I still had something solid beneath me. It lit a fire inside me that I desperately needed at the time, pushing me to work harder, to keep moving forward, and to find a way through everything that was collapsing around me.

The court date arrived, and I had to represent myself. I walked into that courtroom knowing I had nothing but the truth to stand on, but I had no idea how much of a battle it would be. My wife had come prepared, but not with honesty. Apparently, the night before she had called the police, she had bruised her legs in some kind of tantrum. I remembered hearing her moving around, throwing things in the room, but I had no idea she was doing something like this. Whether someone gave her this idea or she came up with it on her own, I didn't know. What I did know was that she presented the court with photos of bruises on her legs, blaming them on me and claiming I had physically abused her in an altercation that never took place.

I was floored.

I told the judge my truth, pointing out that my wife wasn't even home after the police had left and that by the time she got back, I was already asleep. If this supposed altercation had happened before the police arrived, wouldn't she have told them that night? But the judge wasn't swayed easily—I needed proof.

Frantically scrolling through my phone, I searched for anything to prove she was lying. And then, I found it. Pictures I had taken of the family at the lake, my wife paddle boarding shortly before she asked for a divorce. A close-up shot of her sitting on her paddle board, and right there, bruises all over her legs. Bruises that were in the exact same places as the ones she was blaming on me.

I immediately brought this to the judge's attention. I handed over the pictures and asked the judge to compare them to the ones my wife's court-appointed attorney had submitted. It didn't take long for the judge to see straight through her lies.

Her attorney quickly asked for a continuance. Since I wasn't legally represented, the judge granted it—but not before allowing me supervised visitation with my sons every other weekend. A new hearing was scheduled for a permanent parenting plan and child support to be set.

Walking out of that courtroom, I felt something I hadn't felt in a long time—hope.

It wasn't the ideal situation. Supervised visitation wasn't what I wanted, but it was a start. I was going to see my kids, and she had no say over it. That alone was a victory.

Despite winning in court that day, I knew the next battle was already looming. I needed an attorney, and I needed to figure out how I was going to handle child support. I needed more money, and I needed it fast.

But that was tomorrow's problem.

Today, I won.

Small victories mattered when you were fighting for your life. They came few and far between, so I had to celebrate them when they happened.

When I got back to my dad's, I told him the good news, and I could see the relief on his face. It felt good to share something positive after everything I had put him through.

That night, we went out for wings, and I told him everything over dinner.

For the first time in what felt like forever, the was something to celebrate. My dad was proud of me, and I was proud of myself.

Momentum was shifting in my favor, and I fully intended on riding this wave as far as it would take me.

I showed up to my first supervised visitation full of confidence and excitement to finally see my sons again. This wasn't just another visit—this was my opportunity to show my wife that I wasn't broken, that I wasn't the man she expected to find after everything she had put me through. I pulled up in the truck my dad had given me, wearing new clothes that she'd never seen me in before, a fresh haircut, and a new cologne that she hadn't picked out for me.

I needed her to see me at my best.

Without saying a word, I wanted to send a clear message: This time, you're not going to win. You're not going to break me.

She was clearly confused. She looked full of questions but said nothing. I could see the irritation behind her eyes, but I paid her no mind. I completely ignored her and focused solely on my sons.

From the moment I walked in, I made it my mission to make that visit as enjoyable as possible for them. I wanted them to leave with a positive memory of me, something real that no lie could ever replace. With them being so young and so impressionable, I had no idea what was being told to them behind my back. I didn't know how I was being portrayed or if they were being fed narratives that painted me as someone I wasn't. But in that room, during that time, I had the opportunity to show them the truth for themselves.

Everything was going well. The visit was full of laughter, playtime, and bonding moments that I had desperately missed. Then, out of nowhere, my youngest son, accidentally called me by another man's name.

At first, I tried to ignore it. Maybe I misheard him. Maybe it wasn't what I thought.

But then, he said it again.

This time, he said it loudly.

The name cut through the air, ringing out like an alarm that couldn't be silenced.

My wife's face immediately changed. The way she tensed, the way she looked away instead of meeting my eyes—it told me everything I needed to know.

I didn't even have to ask. But I did anyway.

"You already bringing random guys around our kids so soon?" I asked, my voice even but firm.

She ignored me. No explanation, no justification, nothing. Just silence.

That silence said more than words ever could.

A wave of emotions hit me all at once—anger, betrayal, frustration, sadness. But I refused to let any of it show in front of my sons. No matter what I was feeling inside, I wouldn't let her ruin this time with them. I pushed my emotions aside, refocused, and made sure to end the visit on a high note.

As I said my goodbyes, I made sure they knew how much I loved them. I reminded them that I missed them and that I would see them again soon.

But the moment I got in my truck and started driving back to my dad's, my mind went into overdrive.

Who was this guy?

She was clearly bringing him around enough for our youngest son to start saying his name naturally. That meant he had been around for a while.

Was he just visiting? Or had she already moved him in?

Had she been seeing him before she asked for a divorce?

Was this the real reason she left?

The questions wouldn't stop. They ran through my mind like wildfire, and the more I thought about it, the more I knew—I needed answers.

I needed to know the truth.

After years of avoiding social media, I found myself pulled back in.

When everything happened in 2009, I had deleted all of my accounts and kept it that way for a long time. The rare times I gave it another shot, it always seemed to bring more negativity into my life than anything beneficial, so I walked away from it again and again. But now, things were different.

Now, it was just me. And for the first time in a long time, I was truly alone.

At first, I told myself I was just getting back on to reconnect with old friends and follow sports news. I made an Instagram, a Facebook, and a Twitter. Twitter had always been a safe space for me—just sports updates, nothing personal. Facebook reconnected me with family and old friends. And Instagram reignited my love for photography. I started taking pictures again, editing them, and finding joy in capturing moments in a way I hadn't in years.

But then, the algorithms did what they do best.

First, it was Facebook. Do you know this person?

My wife's face popped up on my screen.

Nope. Block.

Then, Instagram did the same.

I hesitated this time. I clicked.

It didn't take long to catch up on everything I had missed. My wife had been going out, dressing up, and posting frequently. She was basking in the attention, especially from other men. She looked different—polished, curated. It wasn't the woman I had been married to for the last decade. There was a strange secrecy about it all, even though she was being very public. No posts of the kids. No acknowledgment of our marriage ending.

And then, I saw something that made my blood boil.

Photos I had taken of her, repurposed with cryptic captions—subtle but intentional. They painted a picture, one I knew wasn't real. She was hinting at being in an abusive relationship. She had been setting this up for months, framing herself as the victim long before she even asked for the divorce.

I shared all of this with Joe, one of my closest friends. He knew my wife well, had been around for our entire marriage, and he couldn't believe what she was doing either. The more we looked, the more it felt like she had completely unraveled.

"Bro, something is seriously wrong with her," Joe said, scrolling through her posts. "Either she's having a mental breakdown or she's on something."

We both shook our heads in disbelief.

Then, Joe noticed something I had missed.

There was one account—one guy—that consistently liked and commented on all of her posts. His profile was private, barely any posts, but the name stood out.

It was the same name our youngest son had said during our visit.

Joe was convinced this was the guy. I wasn't so sure. My mind was fixated on someone else—a guy I swore my wife had met up with weeks before she asked for the divorce.

The same guy she'd dated in Florida during one of our separations down there. He just so happened to be in Chattanooga at the same time she went to visit her old friend there over the weekend. When I confronted her about it, she had brushed it off, acted like I was overreacting, like I was just being a jealous husband.

But I knew better.

Not long after, I came home from work early one day and noticed a water bottle sitting on the counter. It was a brand my wife hated. Nobody in our house drank that water.

I asked her, casually at first, if anyone had been over. She said no.

I ruled out every possible reason why that bottle could be there. I asked if she had bought it from the store. She said no.

So I held it up. "Then whose water bottle is this?"

She froze. Then, she looked me dead in the eyes and said, "It's yours."

That was the moment I knew.

Someone had been at my house. Someone who shouldn't have been.

Fast forward to now, I was convinced he was the guy. Not this random dude Joe was pointing out. The one I had suspected all along.

Joe disagreed.

"Nah, man. I'm telling you, it's this other guy," he insisted. "It's the same dude my son said."

But I let my emotions take over.

I found the guy I suspected on Instagram and sent him a message—one that wasn't exactly polite.

No response. Just a block.

It was frustrating. I had played right into my wife's game. The more attention I gave to this, the more she seemed to feed off of it. It was like she was enjoying the reaction.

I needed to let it go.

I had no control over what she was doing. I couldn't change it. I couldn't stop it. I couldn't undo the damage she had already done.

But what I could control?

Whether or not I gave her the satisfaction of paying attention.

I deleted everything I had just looked at. I blocked her account. I made a promise to Joe right then and there: "Don't show me anything else about her. I don't want to see it. I don't want to know."

And that day, I made another promise to myself.

I was going to become the best version of me possible.

I started posting again—but not out of pettiness, not out of revenge. Every post I made was a reflection of me at my best. Whether it was getting back into shape, doing things I had never done before, or simply proving to myself that I could rise from the ashes my wife had left me in.

I wanted her to see me winning.

Because I knew she was watching.

And the best revenge?

Was success.

With the court battle behind me, I threw myself into the next step—rebuilding.

I had a plan, I had the motivation, and most importantly, I had the determination to never let myself end up in the same position again.

One of the best decisions I made during this time was linking up with my coworker, Juan. He was in immaculate shape, and I wanted to get there. I had already been working long hours and balancing my side hustle, but I squeezed the gym into my routine.

Wake up early, work my side hustle, head to my main job, hit the gym afterward.

The grind was relentless, but the results were undeniable. The weight I had put on during my marriage started to shed. Muscle definition returned. My confidence grew. And with that newfound confidence came a level of social ease that I hadn't felt in years.

I was becoming me again.

But there was still one more battle to face—my first official visit with my sons.

It was supposed to be simple. The court had outlined everything. We were set to exchange at the police station. But when my wife arrived, she refused to give me the boys.

Her reasoning? I didn't have car seats.

I was furious. The car seats in her van were bought by me— we were supposed to share. But my wife, being who she is, used every opportunity to make things as difficult as possible.

She abruptly left the police station, and I was left standing there, stunned.

I went inside and explained everything to an officer. He wasn't surprised. He called her, threatening to put a warrant out for her arrest if she didn't return with the boys.

Her response? "He doesn't have car seats."

The officer, who had clearly seen situations like this before, told me he understood. He even offered to purchase me some cheap car seats himself if I couldn't afford them. I thanked him but declined. Instead, I rushed to Walmart, grabbed what I needed, and returned just in time for her to pull back in.

Finally, I had my sons.

I took them to my dad's, and from that moment on, I made every visit count.

Each time they came over, I had new gifts waiting for them. We played at the park, went to the movies—anything that would bring them joy. They started looking forward to our weekends together, and my dad loved every second of it, playing Grandpa, wrestling with them, and soaking in the time we had.

Seeing their happiness did something to me.

One day, while watching them play, I realized—this is what life was about. Not dwelling on the past. Not worrying about my wife. Not letting the darkness pull me back in.

It was time for the next step.

I talked to my dad about traveling again.

"I need to do this," I told him. "It's always been something that made me happy. I need to find that happiness again."

He understood. In fact, he even talked about going with me on certain trips.

I hit up Joe, asking if he wanted to join me for a quick getaway.

"Oh yeah," he said. "I could definitely use a vacation. Where are we going?"

We settled on Gulf Shores, Alabama—somewhere I had never been before. A quick road trip, right by the beach. Exactly what I needed.

With the extra money I was making, I rented an Airbnb on the river, got a rental car, and picked up the boys. My wife was instantly curious.

"Daddy, why do you have this car?" my oldest son asked.

"It's a surprise," I said, grinning.

She stood there, watching, clearly dying to ask questions but holding herself back.

On the drive back to my dad's, I told the boys the plan.

"We're taking a road trip," I said. "We're going to the beach."

Their excitement was unmatched.

Seeing that joy on their faces did something to me. Changed something in me.

In that moment, I made a silent promise to myself—I would do whatever it took to keep that smile on their faces for the rest of their lives.

The trip to Gulf Shores was incredible.

For me, it was a reset. For Joe, it was an awakening.

"This is what we need to be doing, man," he said. "We're not tied to this place. We can go anywhere, whenever we want."

He was right. The possibilities were endless.

I posted pictures and videos from the trip, documenting the happiness I had found in traveling again. I wasn't just existing anymore—I was living.

But my wife? She clearly didn't like it.

At first, she started making small talk at exchanges, subtly trying to draw me into conversation. When that didn't work, she got flirtatious. I ignored it.

Then, when she saw my posts, she changed.

She demanded I stop traveling with the boys.

I pointed out that the court allowed it.

"Fine," she snapped. "But I want all details upfront. Before you do anything, you tell me first."

I complied. Not because she told me to, but because I wasn't giving her anything to use against me.

Joe and I planned the next trip—this time to Gatlinburg for a fall weekend in the mountains with the boys. Everything was set. I was thriving.

Then, one day, everything changed.

At one of our drop-offs, I noticed something different about my wife.

For weeks, she had been wearing hoodies and baggy shirts. I hadn't thought anything of it.

But on this day, she wasn't.

Her stomach was showing.

And it was poking out.

I felt the words leave my mouth before I could stop them.

"Are you pregnant?"

She smirked but said nothing.

"I'm serious. We're still legally married. Are you seriously pregnant again?"

"That's none of your business," she said coldly.

I stared at her, stunned.

We had just gone through all of this with her daughter before. She knew how difficult that process was.

And now, here she was—doing it again.

Then, it hit me.

I had been ignoring the divorce process, assuming she would take care of it since she was the one who wanted it. It wasn't like I was planning on getting remarried anytime soon, so I just let it sit.

But now?

Now, things were different.

By law, if she was still married to me, then this baby was legally mine until proven otherwise.

She knew this.

She planned this.

This wasn't an accident—this was on purpose.

I felt that all too familiar sinking feeling in my stomach...

My wife's behavior wasn't just toxic.

It was becoming dangerous, again.

CHAPTER 15

FINAL DECREE OF DIVORCE

My wife's pregnancy hit me harder than I ever expected. I had been through three pregnancies with her, and each time, I had fallen deeper in love with her. Those experiences created a bond between us that I thought was unbreakable. Seeing her pregnant again—this time under these circumstances, by someone else, while still married to me—was like a dagger straight to my heart.

It wasn't just the fact that she had moved on so quickly. It was the way she did it. This felt intentional, like a move in some twisted game she was playing. She had been so angry that I wasn't reacting to her anymore, wasn't engaging in her usual chaos, so she made a move that she knew would force me back into her world. A move she knew I couldn't ignore.

I lost a lot of sleep over it. The thoughts consumed me. How could someone be this selfish? This wasn't just about her or me, or whoever she was with now. She was bringing a child into the world under the worst possible circumstances, adding another layer of instability to an already broken situation. And what about the kids she already had? While she was wrapped up in this pregnancy, the children who needed her attention were now an afterthought. My sons were growing up without their mother fully present, and because of the situation she had created, I couldn't be there every day to pick up the slack. It killed me inside.

I finally sent my wife a message, telling her she needed to file for divorce. I made it clear that if I had to file, things would be a lot more complicated, especially with her being pregnant. We needed to do this the right way so we didn't have to go through the same nightmare we had with her daughter years before. She assured me she planned to file, but I had no faith in her words. She had lied too many times before, and I couldn't trust a single thing she said.

She took every opportunity to flaunt her pregnancy in front of me. She knew how much it affected me, and I could see in her eyes that she loved knowing she had found something that got to me. No matter how much I tried to ignore it, there was no way for it not to hurt. This wasn't just about jealousy. It was about betrayal, wasted years, and the realization of just how much time, effort, and love I had poured into someone who never truly valued it.

I hated that it still affected me. Everyone close to me couldn't understand why it still mattered. They told me I should be relieved to be done with her, to move on with my life. And I understood where they were coming from, but the reality was, love doesn't just vanish overnight. You don't just flip a switch and erase a decade of your life, no matter how toxic it was.

At this point, I felt something I had never fully felt before—hatred. I had never hated my wife, no matter what she had done. I had been disappointed, betrayed, heartbroken—but never hateful. But now? Now I could feel it growing inside me, taking root with every interaction, every smug glance, every reminder of the time I had wasted.

And yet, underneath all of it, was the deeper truth I had never faced. She wasn't just my wife—she had become my last hope for love. I had lost Jenny in the most tragic way imaginable, and I had spent years trying to outrun that pain, trying to force myself to believe that I could rebuild something just as real, just as deep, with someone else. And now, I had to face the cold, brutal truth.

I had fought with everything I had to hold on to that love, to save my family.

And I lost.

Because I was the only one fighting.

I had spent months trying to sort through everything the best I could, leaning heavily on friends and family for support. Joe, more than anyone, probably had the clearest perspective on the situation, given everything he had seen unfold. One day, he asked if it was okay to share something he had come across. He didn't want to upset me any further, but he thought it was important.

I told him yes.

That's when he let me know that she had gone public with her relationship. The guy he had suspected all along—the same name my son had mentioned at the visitation—was now openly posted all over her social media. It wasn't just casual posts either. They were full-fledged in a relationship, and she had moved in with him.

I didn't think the pain could cut any deeper, but it did.

Joe told me she was clearly making a spectacle of it, as if she wanted me to see. She had even taken a new family portrait—with my sons—while still legally married to me. The thought of another man standing where I stood, holding my children like they were his, felt like a gut punch I wasn't prepared for. It was one thing to move on, but to erase me like I never existed? To pretend our decade together never happened? To put our sons in the middle of it?

That was cold.

Joe even showed me some of her recent posts where she had taken the opportunity to drag my name through the mud. Publicly. Painting herself as the victim, rewriting history, making it seem like she had been the one who suffered through me, rather than the other way around. It made me sick to my stomach.

That was it. Enough was enough.

I immediately started pressing her harder for the divorce. There was no more playing games, no more waiting for her to decide when she was ready. I told her as soon as she filed the papers, I would sign them and send them in immediately. I don't know if she was actually ready for this either, but at this point, it didn't matter. She had made her bed, and now she had to lie in it.

Eventually, the official complaint for divorce was hand-delivered to my dad's front door.

This was it.

I took the paperwork, sat down, and read every word from beginning to end. Then, my eyes locked onto the blank line above the word Signature—my name staring back at me.

I couldn't do it.

Not that night.

I fell asleep on a damp pillow, the tears coming despite how much I tried to hold them back. No matter how much I hated her, no matter how badly I wanted to move on, this still hurt like hell.

The next morning, I woke up and read through the paperwork again. It stated that everything would stay the same with the parenting plan, and that was all I needed to see. I grabbed a pen and signed my name. I didn't let my emotions settle in. I focused on the anger instead. I grabbed my keys, got in my truck, and drove straight to the courthouse in Murfreesboro to turn it in.

There was no hesitation.

It was done.

We were done. Ten years, gone.

I sat in my truck outside the courthouse for what felt like an eternity, feeling every emotion rush over me. There was sadness, anger, regret, relief—but there was also something else. Something unexpected.

Peace.

I didn't trust it, not yet. But I acknowledged it.

On my way home, I called Joe and told him I had signed the papers and turned them in. I told him I didn't want to hear any more updates about her. I didn't care what she was doing, who she was with, or what she posted online. Unless it had something to do with my kids, it was no longer my concern.

There was a cooling-off period before the final decree of divorce would be issued. After that, she and I would be legally over. For good.

It was time to shift my focus back to myself.

And turn the page on me and her for good.

At first, the transition was extremely hard. I had to finally accept that I was no longer a husband in a marriage with kids and a full-time father. Saying goodbye to that portion of my life was an extremely difficult process. I had become so accustomed to being that guy—being okay with that identity—that officially letting it go felt unsettling. I was also not in my twenties anymore. The single life was going to be very different now, and I had no idea what to expect.

Rather than diving into the unknown, I quickly decided that I wasn't going to seek out anything in that direction. If something came to me, it came, but I wasn't going to pursue it. Instead, I threw myself back into the gym, reconnected with friends and family, and focused on traveling—things that had always brought me joy and a sense of fulfillment. More than anything, I maximized my time with my sons, making every visit a priority and creating the best memories possible with them along the way.

With my mind set on forward momentum, my next major goal was to get my own place. I needed something stable, something that was mine, where I could raise my boys and build the next chapter of my life on my terms. God must have seen my struggle, because just when I least expected it, I was presented with something I hadn't even considered—a house. Not just an apartment or a townhome, but the possibility of our own house for me and my sons to call our home.

While waiting for the house to be ready, I could excitedly shift my focus back to self-improvement, knowing that a place to call my own was officially in the works. My attitude had shifted at work and everywhere else in general to a much more positive and upbeat demeanor that I had been known for. I was starting to feel like myself again, and it showed. I found myself socializing a lot more in and outside of work, and my confidence was growing as the work I was putting in at the gym was starting to show more and more.

Women that I worked with and saw at the gym regularly were now striking up conversations with me, and I found myself easily flirting and conversing back. This led to a lot of exchanging of numbers and socials. I started getting myself more involved with new people and, especially, new women. This behavior started opening up windows of opportunity for dates outside of work. It felt brand new, but it felt good.

I eventually started hitting it off with a girl at my job, and we shared a lot of similar interests. I made it very clear that I wasn't looking for anything serious, but I welcomed any new friendships. This stance seemed cool with her, and we began hanging out and talking more outside of work.

Easter was coming up, and I wanted to plan a trip to the beach for my sons for Easter weekend, but I couldn't find anyone else who wanted to go. I spoke to her about going but mentioned it could possibly be a handful if I did it myself. She offered to help if I was comfortable with that. I let her know that it would be strictly platonic and that I was not trying to make it into anything more than that. She was completely understanding upfront and still willing to help. We set it up, and a beach trip was planned.

Everything went well—from the trip there to the stay and the trip back. We seemed to really click, sharing our taste in music and other things, and she did really well with the boys. She was completely respectful on the trip, keeping it strictly platonic as I had asked. Since we worked together, our conversations continued, and eventually, we took that relationship to the next level.

We started dating and everything seemed to be going well but reality started to set in and everything was moving too fast for me. It got a bit overwhelming, I was enjoying myself and her company and having a new woman in my life definitely took the edge off of my encounters with my ex wife but I could feel something shifting in her the more we would date and it wasn't with me so I felt the need to slow it down. I expressed this to her, but she shared that she was growing more attached to me over time. I could tell we weren't really seeing eye to eye with where things were, but I reluctantly continued talking and hanging out with her nonetheless.

I had a trip coming up with Joe to Gatlinburg with the boys, but we were already setting up a new trip to Miami after that. This time, it would include Joe, Juan, Joe's brother Kendrick, and the girl I was dating. Everyone seemed to have their reservations about her coming along, considering they knew where I was with my relationship with her and how I felt the need to slow it down. They warned that if I took her with us, I was doing the exact opposite and giving her the wrong impression, regardless of what I was saying. She clearly wanted more, and if I gave more to her, I was sending the wrong signal.

I knew they were right, and I knew I had to do something about it, but I didn't want to cause any problems, especially since we worked together. Welcome to the single life, Keith... life comes at you fast. This was the last thing I wanted to be dealing with, but I wanted to get back to where I was. I knew I had to break things off, there was no other option.

I spent a lot of time running different scenarios in my head, trying to figure out the best way to handle the situation, but the truth was, I had made a mistake from the start. Getting involved with her while working together was a bad decision—one I knew deep down, but I had ignored the signs. I was fresh out of a marriage, still broken, and in no position to be in a relationship, especially with someone who clearly wanted more than I could give.

There was no way to make this easy. The best thing to do was to be direct, so I asked to speak with her face-to-face. I explained where I stood, letting her know I wasn't ready for anything serious and that I still valued our friendship, but I also knew how hollow those words probably sounded to her. She wasn't taking it well, and nothing I said seemed to soften the blow. She felt like I had been leading her on. From my perspective, I had been upfront about my intentions, but looking back, my actions sent mixed signals, and she had every right to feel hurt.

Things between us soured almost immediately at work. She had already paid for her part of the Miami trip, and though I offered a full refund, it wasn't enough. She still wanted to go, but I knew that wasn't an option. I gave her the refund against her wishes, and that's when things took a hard turn.

One night, while I was closing with Juan, she left work early. When I walked out to my truck, I found food thrown all over it. I knew it was her. It was a petty, emotional reaction, but it caught me off guard. I confronted her about it, telling her it was unnecessary and that I had been through enough toxic situations before to know I wasn't about to deal with another one. I warned her that if she pulled something like that again, she'd be dealing with legal consequences.

That was the last I saw of her—she never returned to work. It was an ugly, unnecessary mess, but it was a lesson I wouldn't forget. I told myself I wouldn't put myself in that position again.

I quickly shifted my focus back to the Miami trip. This trip was going to be special—a place I had always dreamed of visiting, and I was going to do it with my boys. A guys' trip. This was going to be awesome, and I couldn't wait. It was everything I imagined it to be and more. We had a blast, visiting every possible hot spot in Miami and even driving down to the Keys. I had always wanted to experience South Florida, so this was a dream come true.

I completely let loose. It felt good to be back in this position again, and I vowed to myself—not in Miami, not anywhere—would I rush into love again. I was going to enjoy life with my friends and my sons. I took endless pictures and videos, made edits galore, and posted them all on social media, having a blast doing it. It was long overdue. I had dedicated my entire twenties to a marriage that had stolen everything from me, so I wasn't about to let my thirties slip away.

While in Miami, we started planning our next trip—this time to San Diego. We were headed to the West Coast soon, floating on cloud nine. I began to realize that seeing my ex wife was having less of an effect on me because I had so much positivity going on in my life. I was getting into the best shape of my life, traveling to places I had always dreamed of visiting, and doing it all with my friends and my sons while waiting for my new house to be ready. It was pure bliss.

But life has a funny way of knocking you back down to earth. Amid all the positivity, I came home to a manila envelope tucked into my door. Final Decree of Divorce was written at the top of the paperwork. I took a deep breath, closed my eyes for a moment, and slid the paperwork back into the envelope. That chapter of my life was officially behind me.

I placed the envelope into my filing folder with the intent of never pulling it out again. It was time to move on. I wasn't looking back—I was only moving forward. I owed it to myself and my sons to become the best version of me possible, and that day, I promised myself I would make sure of it.

CHAPTER 16

A LIFE OF OUR OWN

The age-old saying 'time flies when you're having fun' was an understatement. Before I knew it, my house was ready to move into. I was excited and nervous at the same time—my entire adult life had been spent in apartments, where maintenance was just a phone call away. Now, every responsibility would fall on my shoulders, and that was going to be a learning curve. But I was ready.

I had saved up a good amount of money to furnish the house properly, so the first few weeks were spent organizing, moving in furniture, and making it feel like home. The boys were beside themselves with excitement, having their own rooms for the first time. At their mom's, they often complained about not having enough space, but here, they could run around and play freely. Their bedroom was spacious, and they each got to pick their own themed beds—My oldest son chose Cars, and my youngest son went with Paw Patrol. The look on their faces when we set up their beds together and I tucked them in for the first time was priceless. My oldest son loved his so much that he barely wanted to leave it.

One night, after putting them to bed, I stood in the dining room, looking around at the house, imagining all the possibilities. A deep sense of accomplishment washed over me. I had come a long way from that day in Murfreesboro with just a garbage bag full of clothes. Now, I had a home, two vehicles in the driveway, and my sons asleep in their own rooms. I closed my eyes, took a deep breath, and thanked God for everything He had blessed me with.

Things started coming together nicely, and my sister Leeanne, always the creative and crafty one, wanted to help decorate and make the house feel even more like home. She took on several projects, building a coffee bar in the dining room, custom bunk beds for the boys, a full-size kitchen table big enough for the whole family, and even transforming the second family room into a playroom with a two-story reading nook where the boys could sleep if they wanted a movie night campout. She decorated the entire home in a way that reflected my personality, even scattering framed photos from my travels around the house, giving me constant reminders of the good times.

Meanwhile, our next big trip was approaching—this time, to Los Angeles. I invited my sister to join us as a thank-you for all her hard work, but she was hesitant since her daughter's birthday was coming up. I suggested bringing her daughter along, and when she mentioned that her stepdaughter was visiting too, I invited her as well. To show my appreciation, I covered a lot of the expenses. Eventually, she agreed, and we set off on what became one of the best trips I'd ever been on. We made countless memories, took tons of pictures—some of which still hang on my walls today—and had an amazing time. Having my sister along for this trip meant a lot to me; it was something I never imagined would be possible at this point in my life.

During the LA trip, a conversation sparked between my sister and me about my work and side jobs. I had one paid vacation left at my main job, and I always wondered—what if I dedicated the same time I spent at my full-time job to my side business? Could I match my income, or maybe even surpass it? I was terrified of taking that leap, but after multiple conversations with my sister, Joe, and Juan, they encouraged me to go for it.

Shortly after returning from LA, a dispute with my boss over pay and time off sealed my decision. I was simply tired of answering to someone else, tired of having my schedule and my income controlled by others. I took my final vacation and used that time to work my side jobs full-time. By the end of the week, I had not only matched my regular income but exceeded it. After careful budgeting and planning, I put in my two weeks' notice. Halfway through serving it, I decided to walk away for good. From that moment forward, I only answered to myself. It was one of the best decisions I ever made.

This transition freed up more time than I ever had before. I was able to spend more time with my sons and plan even more trips with friends and family. By this point, the travel bug had fully taken hold, and I had visited Miami, San Diego, Los Angeles, Denver, the Smoky Mountains, and various places in Florida—including two unforgettable trips to Disney World with my sons. Those Disney trips were special, not only because I had never been before, but because I was able to provide that magical experience for my boys while they were still young enough to fully appreciate it. My sister and nephew even joined us on one of the trips, making it even more special.

With all this traveling, my friend Julian started encouraging me to try international travel. He had taken several trips abroad and spoke highly of the experiences. The idea of traveling internationally made me nervous, but I was open to it. Around this time, I also started thinking about dating again. My life was finally aligning in a way that made me feel ready to put myself back out there.

That's when I heard about Tinder. I had single friends who mentioned it in passing, so I decided to give it a shot. I made a profile, matched with a few girls, but nothing really stuck. One night, while watching a movie on my couch, I got a notification—someone had sent me a Super Like. I had no idea what that was. When I opened the notification, I saw a picture of a stunning Latina named Gabriela.

I was immediately intrigued. As I scrolled through her pictures and read her profile, I saw that she lived in Mexico. Why would someone from Mexico Super Like my profile? It didn't make sense. I thought Tinder was location-based, and I hadn't been anywhere near Mexico except for a short time in San Diego months ago. Still, I figured there was no harm in messaging her.

To my surprise, she responded the next morning, and our conversation flowed effortlessly. We shared many common interests, and she explained that she was using Tinder Passport because she planned on moving to the U.S. When I asked her why she chose to Super Like me, her answer caught me off guard.

She told me that I was exactly the type of man she was looking for. She had seen the picture of me and my sons, and what truly stood out to her was the way they looked at me. She said she could tell they loved and admired me, and to her, that meant I was a good father and a good man. That was what triggered her to Super Like me.

I was flattered, and my curiosity grew. As we continued talking, I told her about my interest in trying international travel, and she brought up the idea of visiting Mexico. Before long, I was planning my first international trip—to Cancun—a four day weekend getaway where Gabriela and I could meet in person for the first time and see where things went from there.

While planning for the trip to Cancun, I was at work one day, driving around and talking to Joe when he brought up the fact that a new documentary was coming out about everything that had happened in 2009 with Jenny and Steve McNair. The moment he mentioned it, I felt my stomach drop. Over the years, production companies had reached out to me, asking me to take part in their projects covering that story, but I had always ignored them. After the way I was treated by CBS Investigates and how they handled that interview, I wanted nothing to do with anything like that again. The idea of another documentary being released without my input made me uneasy, but I tried to keep my focus on the trip ahead.

Joe, however, explained that this was different. He sounded serious, even a little concerned. It wasn't just another short segment or a news piece—it was a full-length audio documentary, a podcast that would be featured on Spotify, and it was being done by Sports Illustrated. He told me it was going to cover all the questionable details surrounding the case, giving it the kind of in-depth attention it had never fully received before. Hearing that Sports Illustrated was behind it gave me pause. This wasn't just some minor production; this was a major publication diving into the details of my past.

I was intrigued, but I also remembered that months prior, someone from Sports Illustrated had reached out to me. At the time, I assumed it was just for an article or a minor feature, so I dismissed it. I had no idea they were creating a full-on documentary. But now, it was already completed and on its way to being released.

The thought of everything being dragged back into the spotlight made me uneasy. I had been doing so well mentally and emotionally, and I felt like I had finally reached a good place in my life—almost as if I had found some form of closure. My focus had been on building a new life, transitioning into a new line of work, traveling, and being the best father I could be to my sons. I had reestablished control over my life, and for the first time in a long time, I felt truly free from the weight of my past.

Unfortunately, I was very wrong. That sense of peace was about to be tested in ways I hadn't anticipated.

I tried my best to keep the Sports Illustrated documentary out of sight and out of mind. Things were going well in my life, and I didn't want anything to deter me from that. I had been through this before, and I kept reminding myself that I could make it through it again. It had almost become an annual routine—every July, there would be another story popping up somewhere about what happened in 2009. But I knew this one was different. In the back of my mind, I worried about how they would tell the story. Without my personal input, they could portray me however they wanted, and the last thing I needed was another wave of people attacking me online.

I shifted my focus back to the Cancun trip, venting a little to Gabriela about everything. She helped keep my mind off of it and redirected my thoughts to the positives in my life. I appreciated that about her. As the trip got closer, I could feel my nerves building. It had been easy talking to Gabriela over the phone and even over video chat, but meeting in person was a different story. I had been completely honest with Gabriela about everything from the very beginning. She knew my history, the ups and downs, the highs and lows. I left no stone unturned because I wanted her to understand who I was completely before she decided if she wanted to take things any further. But rather than scare her off, it seemed to pull her in even closer.

When I arrived in Cancun, I was blown away. I had been to countless beaches in Florida, but nothing quite compared to this. The water was an unreal shade of blue, and the entire atmosphere had a different kind of energy. It was like a dream.

When I reached the spot where I was supposed to meet Gabriela, I spotted her standing there in black shades, scanning the crowd for me. She looked even better than in her pictures. Then she saw me. Without hesitation, she ran toward me and jumped into my arms. I didn't even have time to anticipate how our first kiss would go—she kissed me immediately, and it was perfect. That instant chemistry shot my attraction to her up several levels. She took my hand and confidently led the way. I loved that trait in a woman—someone who didn't need a man to guide her but could take charge when she wanted to. Jenny had that quality too. It was something I had always been drawn to.

Once we got in the car, the conversation flowed naturally. Her English was broken, my Spanish was rusty, but we still managed to connect effortlessly. When we arrived at the resort, I quickly unpacked. It was even better than I had imagined—luxurious and vibrant, with stunning ocean views. After a little time winding down in the room, Gabriela's energy kicked back in, and she was eager to explore.

The resort itself was amazing, but when we made our way down to the beach, I was speechless. The view was breathtaking. I knew this weekend was going to be incredible, and Gabriela's adventurous spirit was going to make it even better.

We made the most of every moment. She had an itinerary mapped out in her head, and I let her take the lead. Normally, I liked to be in control of my plans, but this time, I was having so much fun going along with hers that I saw no reason to change a thing. We captured some of the coolest pictures and videos I had ever taken. Being with Gabriela reignited my love for photography and videography.

We didn't just stay at the resort—we took day trips, including an unforgettable visit to Chichen Itza to explore the ancient ruins and swim in a cenote waterfall. It was surreal. Everything about this trip felt like a dream come true, and I had Gabriela to thank for it.

The weekend flew by, and four days felt more like two. Before I knew it, we were saying our goodbyes. Gabriela had tears in her eyes as she insisted on planning another trip. I promised I would come back, and we decided on Cabo for our next destination. That's when she told me she wanted to be with me and that she was going to do everything in her power to get to the U.S. as quickly as possible. I had no experience in immigration matters, so I had to take her word for it. Before I left, she asked me for one more thing—she wanted us to be exclusive, no matter the distance.

It didn't take much thought. I had no plans of dating anyone else, and I hadn't even been looking when Gabriela came along. I gave her my word, kissed her goodbye, and boarded my flight back to Nashville, officially in a long-distance relationship—something I had never tried before.

When I got back, I filled everyone in on how well the trip had gone. I encouraged Joe and the others I traveled with to visit Cancun with me sometime. Most people were supportive of Gabriela, though there was an understandable amount of skepticism. I'm sure Gabriela and I both had our own doubts in the back of our minds as well. A long-distance relationship was unfamiliar territory, but since I knew I was going back, I figured there was no harm in giving it a shot. Cancun had gone so well—who knew? Maybe this could actually work.

Time passed, and eventually, the Sports Illustrated documentary was released episode by episode. I told myself I wasn't going to listen, but I broke. Every episode that passed, I was impressed. They were telling the story well, covering details that others had ignored. They seemed to be heading in the right direction, and I was pleasantly surprised.

That is, until the episode titled The Ex-Boyfriend and the Ex-Convict aired.

I listened, and while I wasn't shocked by how they portrayed me, I was disappointed. Even with all the available proof out there, they still painted me in a negative and questionable light. Joe listened as well, and while he agreed this was probably the most thorough coverage anyone had ever done on the case, he was frustrated with the way they framed my role in the story.

After that episode was released I started to get messages from people again regarding the story with questions wanting to be answered since I hadn't spoken up for myself in years.

Talking it over with Joe, I brought up an idea: what if we started a podcast? A place where we could finally tell my story, unfiltered and uncut—without anyone twisting my words or controlling the narrative.

Joe didn't hesitate. "What took you so long?" he said. "I've been ready to do this for years."

That was it. I was done staying silent. Once and for all, it was time to tell my side of the story.

CHAPTER 17

BREAKING THE SILENCE

It only took a few conversations to lay the outline of the podcast, and Joe and I were off to the races. We settled on the name Beyond the Shadows: Overcoming Tragedy. The name resonated with both of us, considering how much we had bottled up over the years and the number of traumatic experiences we had overcome.

With the outline and name decided, we both went out and got all the equipment we needed. Our experience in recording music and building home studios made this process relatively easy. Before long, we were ready to record the first episode.

With the events of 2009 being the catalyst for starting the podcast, we knew we wanted to cover more than just that. Joe and I had both faced numerous challenges throughout our lives, and we assumed many others out there had similar stories. We decided to focus on men's mental health—something we had both battled in silence for years. The goal was to open up, unfiltered, about the most trying moments of our lives.

This was a refreshing experience. We had previously used music as an outlet, pouring our emotions onto paper. Now, we had found a new way to express ourselves, and it felt right.

The first episode did surprisingly well. The feedback was positive, and we quickly gained a few subscribers. Seeing the impact our words had on others gave us the motivation to continue. We didn't jump straight into the situation from 2009, though we knew that moment was coming. Instead, we eased into it, sharing other personal experiences first.

At the time, nobody knew who we were, but we understood that might change once we recorded that episode. I spent days going over it in my mind, thinking about how to approach it the right way. When the time finally came, I told Joe I wanted to go in blind—unscripted.

Joe agreed and prepared a set of questions designed to cover everything, especially the details that other media outlets had conveniently left out.

"You ready?" Joe asked.

I sat in front of my laptop, staring at the screen. I took a deep breath. "Yeah, I'm good. Let's do it." And I pressed record.

Joe had prepared well—his questions were direct but thoughtful. The conversation flowed naturally between us, just like any other day. We had talked about this so many times before that the microphone and monitor soon faded from my awareness. It was just me and Joe, sitting at the table, talking.

I let everything out. If there was emotion behind my words, I didn't hold it back. We kept going, lost in the conversation, until we suddenly realized we had been recording for over two hours.

The reality of the time constraint set in, so we started wrapping things up. Finally, the conversation was over.

"How you feeling?" Joe asked.

I exhaled. "That was a lot to get out, man, but I feel good. I'm glad we did that."

"Yeah, me too," Joe said. "I'm glad you finally had the opportunity to let it all out."

That night, I stayed up editing the episode for our YouTube channel. It was long, so it would take overnight to upload. Finally, it was done and ready to post.

No turning back now, I thought to myself.

I texted Joe to let him know it was done, clicked upload, and went to bed.

I woke up the next morning to see that the episode had been posted successfully and had already started getting views. I texted Joe to let him know it was up so he could check it out when he woke up, then I shared the video with family and friends, asking them to check it out and share their opinions.

That day at work, I felt a mix of nervousness and anticipation. There had been so much negativity surrounding me for years because of that situation, and I instinctively worried that this would bring more of the same. Then the first comment rolled in—someone from Antioch congratulating me on finally sharing my side of the story. Then another, complimenting Joe and me on a job well done with the episode.

Soon, texts and messages started rolling in from friends and family, telling me how proud they were that I had spoken up. The positive feedback was overwhelming. I let Gabriela know the episode was up, and she watched it as well. She told me we had done a great job and was even shocked to learn some details that she hadn't known before. Throughout it all, she remained extremely supportive and encouraged us to keep going.

With all the positivity rolling in, I could finally breathe and relax a little. Even if negativity did come, at least now there was positivity to counterbalance it. A quiet sense of relief washed over me, along with a bit of pride—I had finally let it all out.

For years, I had held onto information that I felt was crucial, details that had been left out or misrepresented. Now, my story was out there, unfiltered, and no one could twist my words. What I believed in my heart remained unchanged—Jenny did not do this. And now, with my side of the story finally in the open, it was up to anyone willing to listen to decide for themselves with all the facts on the table.

As time went by, we noticed the views and comments on our podcast episode started to dwindle. YouTube wasn't pushing the content the way we had hoped, leaving us to rely on people stumbling across it by chance. I tried promoting it on different social media platforms, but most of our audience had already seen it. Sharing clips on TikTok brought in more attention, but while the TikTok clips gained traction, they kept most of the engagement there, not transferring to YouTube.

Joe and I decided it was time to move forward and start recording more episodes, covering other topics. We filmed another episode discussing social anxiety and how it holds people back from success and other aspects of life. Unfortunately, YouTube still wasn't pushing our content, no matter what we did. We tagged everything correctly, ensured all the settings were optimized, but nothing seemed to change. With TikTok performing well, I shifted more focus to creating shorter clips for that platform.

Life started getting in the way of producing our next episode as quickly as we would have liked. Joe's work schedule didn't align well with mine, and with the discouraging performance on YouTube, it wasn't as motivating to carve out extra time to record. Then, out of nowhere, everything changed.

One day, while talking on the phone, Joe decided to check the podcast's email. As he scrolled through, he suddenly stopped, his voice full of shock. "Bro, you're not gonna believe this," he said. "We have an email from Netflix."

I was stunned. Netflix? That was the last thing I expected. Joe read the email aloud. They said they were tied to the Untold documentary series and had watched our podcast episode. They were intrigued by the story and planned to cover Steve McNair's career and death in their new series. They wanted to talk to me, hoping I would be willing to share my side of the story.

I didn't know what to say as Joe read the email. I had never anticipated our podcast gaining this level of recognition. "You need to email them back, bro," Joe said. "This is the opportunity you've been waiting for—to tell your side of the story on a massive platform."

He was right. "Yeah, man, I need to do this," I said.

"I'll let you go. Email them back and let me know if they respond," Joe said. We hung up, and I sat there staring at the words on the screen.

"Hi Keith, hope you are well! We recently came across your podcast, Beyond the Shadows, and we're hoping to connect with you. We work on a sports documentary series called Untold. Each episode airs on Netflix and tells a separate story of a team, athlete, or event. The series gives space for athletes and the people around them to tell their stories from their own point of view. I'll send through a trailer for a couple of the episodes below so you can get a feel for the show:

UNTOLD: Manti Te'o

UNTOLD: Malice at the Palace

We are currently working on an episode that explores Steve McNair's career and death. This story could not be told without covering Jenny's story and the people in her life. This episode is intended to provide more insight into the circumstances surrounding their passing.

The team behind our series works diligently to provide a space for the people actually involved in our episodes to tell their story. We think it's incredibly important, and one of the many reasons we are reaching out to you today. We'd really love to set up a call with you to introduce ourselves and hopefully connect with you more on Jenny and your story.

We look forward to hearing from you."

Wow. Netflix. I had watched every one of their Untold documentaries and admired the way they told their stories. They gave everyone a voice—even those who had been unfairly labeled as villains. If I was going to speak on this level again, these were the right people to do it with.

I took a deep breath and clicked "Reply."

"I apologize for the late response; I was working. I'm very familiar with Untold, and I thought the Manti Te'o special was great. I'm definitely open to talking with you about everything that happened in 2009 with McNair and Jenny. But before we move forward, I want to make one thing clear —I haven't spoken publicly about this in 14 years for a reason.

Back in 2009, I agreed to do an interview with CBS Investigates to defend Jenny and myself, and to provide details that backed my stance on her innocence. At the time, the media was running wild with speculation, and though the police knew my exact whereabouts—having me on video at work well after 3:00 a.m.—they had not publicly confirmed this. The media twisted the narrative, and I found myself being painted in a negative light.

When I did the interview, I was promised it would focus on clearing Jenny's name and my own. They did not keep that promise. Out of a three-hour interview, they clipped it down to ten minutes, twisting my words and making it appear incriminating. After that betrayal, I vowed never to speak publicly about it again, out of respect for Jenny and her family.

I started this podcast with my friend Joe—who was close to Jenny and our relationship—because I finally reached a place in my life where I could comfortably talk about what happened. More importantly, I wanted to help others who may be going through something similar. With my own platform, I could speak freely without fear of manipulation.

If we move forward, I need to know that this will not be an attempt to twist the narrative again. My goal is to show the world that Jenny was not who she was portrayed to be in 2009 and to shed light on the questionable details surrounding how this case was handled. I believe there is a very real possibility that she was innocent, and people deserve to see that side of the story.

I will be working through Saturday but will be available Sunday. Feel free to reach out anytime, and if I'm unable to answer, I'll respond promptly. Thank you for reaching out—I look forward to hearing from you."

Send.

I took a deep breath and tried my best to shift my focus back to work, knowing that would probably be difficult for a while.

It didn't take long for Netflix to reach back out. If I'm not mistaken, it was the very next morning when I received a response. Soon, we were talking on the phone, going over the details of setting up a conference call and an eventual meeting to film. I was nervous and excited at the same time. I hadn't been on screen like that in almost 15 years. Filming in the comfort of my own home and posting it online was one thing, but sitting in front of a camera, knowing that everything I said would be judged by millions, was another. I was thrilled to share my story on the largest platform possible but extremely anxious about how it would be received.

Balancing the emotions of this opportunity alongside what was happening in my personal life was difficult. Things weren't lining up well for Gabriela and me—every avenue we explored for her coming to the U.S. kept falling through. By this point, I had taken multiple trips back to Mexico. One-on-one, we spent an unforgettable Valentine's Day in Cancun, which went so well that we decided to set up another trip for both of our families to meet. For our third trip to Cancun, Gabriela brought her parents, and I brought my sister, her family, and my dad. It was an incredible experience, one that made us even more determined to take our relationship to the next level.

Unfortunately, this was when things started to take a turn for the worse. Gabriela was exhausting every possible visa option, but with the overwhelming backlog at the border and within the immigration system, every attempt either fell through or was delayed indefinitely. The stress of the situation started to weigh on both of us, leading to arguments that we hadn't had before.

Eventually, we planned another trip—this time to Cabo, where Gabriela was working. It was a perfect chance to explore another part of Mexico together, something we had talked about doing for a long time. But when I arrived, I could tell things were different. The stress of immigration setbacks, the lack of time spent together over the past year, and the demands of our individual lives created a tension that hadn't existed before. Arguments became more frequent, and the carefree energy of our past trips was nowhere to be found. Instead of looking forward to a vacation with Gabriela, I found myself looking forward to returning home.

That trip led to our first breakup—something neither of us had anticipated. It was painful, but after everything I had been through before, I immediately shifted my focus back to my sons, my work, and the upcoming filming for the Netflix documentary. Gabriela and I made several attempts to reconcile, and while we managed to find that connection again from a distance, every effort for her to move to the U.S. failed. Over time, our communication faded, and eventually, we stopped talking altogether. I haven't been back to Mexico since.

Time passed, and eventually, it was my turn to film. The production company flew into Nashville and rented out an Airbnb where most of us would be interviewed including myself, Jeff Fisher and Robert Gaddy, Mcnair's former friend and bodyguard and someone I had definitely questioned their actions that day. I took the day off work and drove out to the Airbnb, where I was met by the director and producers of the documentary.

They were all extremely kind and accommodating, which helped ease my nerves. I had no idea how things were going to go, but they gave me a full rundown of the process and did everything they could to make me feel comfortable. It was fascinating to see the behind-the-scenes mechanics of how these documentaries were made—it truly took a whole team to make everything work seamlessly.

As I sat on the couch, the anxiety started to settle in. I tried my best to shake it off, but as the crew made their final preparations, there was no turning back. The room quieted, and the weight of the moment sank in. This was it.

I took a deep breath as the director gave the nod. The silence was palpable—you could hear a pin drop. The cameras started rolling, and then came the first question.

CHAPTER 18

BEYOND THE SHADOWS

With the first question out of the way, I was starting to settle in. Here and there, in between questions, the reality of what I was doing would set in, allowing anxiety to creep back in. But the director did a great job of reeling me back when necessary. I was there for almost eight hours, answering questions and covering every detail about my relationship with Jenny and everything surrounding the case, including all the questionable details and what I truly believed happened.

I was feeling really good about the direction of the interview. The more I felt like the right questions were being asked, the more confident I became in my answers, feeling like this was finally going to be told the right way. As the questions dwindled down, the director told me he had one final question before we wrapped things up. I had done well keeping my emotions in check throughout the entire day, but for some reason, this last question hit me right in the heart and unexpectedly struck a chord with me on another level. It was simple, but I guess I had never really thought about it before.

"If it weren't me sitting right here in front of you and instead it was Jenny, and you had one opportunity to tell her one last thing to her face, what would it be?"

I sat there in silence, trying to comprehend the question. As soon as it hit, there was no holding it back. Tears began to flow, and all the emotion I had worked so hard to contain throughout the day came flooding out. Through the tears, I did my best to answer.

"I would tell her I'm sorry. I'm so sorry from the bottom of my heart for everything, and I wish I could take back the role I played in her life going down the path that it did. I would tell her I miss her every day, whether it's ever said out loud or in silence. And I would tell her I love her. I love her endlessly, from the moment I met her to the moment I take my last breath. I always have and I always will."

I buried my face in my hands as the tears continued to flow and asked for a moment. When I looked up, I noticed the director had tears welling up in his eyes as well. The room was quiet, everyone lost in thought, reflecting on everything that had been said. The cameras were still rolling as I broke the silence. I explained to the director how I felt guilty still being here sometimes. I told him how the best part of my life is being a father and the immense joy I have felt watching my kids grow up, and it tears me apart to know that Jenny never got to experience that.

Me and Jenny used to talk about having kids all the time, and I could see the twinkle in her eye when she spoke about it, but we both assumed we had forever to get there. She never had the opportunity to be a mother, never had the chance to get married, and knowing how it feels to be a parent, it kills me inside that she never got to experience that joy.

The room remained silent as I wiped my tears. The director stood up and opened his arms. "I need to give you a hug, man," he said. "Please, give me a hug. I'm so sorry. I can't even imagine."

I walked over and embraced him, not realizing how much I actually needed that. We said our goodbyes, and I drove home, fixated on that last question. It stayed with me for a long time afterward.

As time passed, I tried to settle back into normalcy. They let me know the documentary would likely be released the following summer. Joe and I talked about continuing the podcast, but the experience had been so emotionally draining that it was hard to get back into the right mindset. With our schedules misaligned, it was easy to keep putting it off, and before we knew it, months had passed. Life took such a different direction after that that Joe and I barely spoke for nearly a year. We had gone through periods like that before, so it wasn't unusual for our friendship.

Unfortunately, my sons were going through difficulties at their mother's house. As they got older, they started sharing more details with me about the bad decisions being made on her end. They became more vocal about wanting to live with me full-time. I had always acknowledged their concerns but had never wanted to take time away from their mother. I underestimated the severity of the situation.

I had never looked into my ex wife's living situation or the choices she was making. She never shared details with me, and I couldn't even get basic medical information about the boys from her. As they became more vocal about their negative experiences, I started paying closer attention. The more I dug, the more questionable everything became. When I tried to confront my ex wife about what the boys were telling me, I was met with confrontation, arguments, and threats to stay out of her business. Over time, their experiences became more concerning, and their desire to live with me never wavered. Eventually, I felt compelled to consult an attorney.

I provided all the details my sons had shared with me, and my attorney insisted that the situation was not okay. I needed to seek full custody. I consulted with my family and spoke with my boys one last time. The last thing I ever wanted to do was pull them away from their mother, but the attorney and my family agreed that it was necessary. My sons remained firm in their decision. After deep consideration, I hired the attorney and filed for full custody.

That decision would pull me and my boys into a battle with their mother worse than anything before—a battle I'm still fighting to this day. In the midst of all this, the documentary had become an afterthought. Then, out of nowhere, I got the call—it was about to air.

The anxiety from the court battle with my ex wife was now joined by the anxiety of how the documentary would be received by the public. I tried to manage both, keeping my head down and focusing on what mattered most. Then they released the trailer for the new Untold season, and my episode was the primary focus. Nearly the entire trailer was centered on my segment. Seeing myself from that perspective was surreal. I was nervous—really nervous—after watching it.

Soon, the calls, texts, and messages started pouring in from all directions. People saw the trailer, and they had questions. I did my best to catch everyone up, but it was overwhelming. When the full documentary was released, I didn't watch it immediately. Instead, I had close family members watch it first, so they could prepare me for what I was about to see.

There were mixed reviews. Some said it was well done, but others were disappointed. They knew all the information I had provided and felt that a lot of it had been left out. I was warned that it contained graphic images from the crime scene that had never been shown before. I had always avoided seeing those images, and I needed to mentally and emotionally prepare myself before watching.

Finally, I watched it. The production quality was excellent, but I quickly realized they barely touched on the questionable material. They skimmed over the key details that could have changed the entire narrative. When my segment came up, I saw how much had been cut. My eight-hour interview had been trimmed down significantly. While I appreciated that they respected my request to leave out certain names, I couldn't ignore the disappointment. This was the one opportunity to truly open people's eyes, but they had chosen to downplay the inconsistencies.

Despite everything, it was done. The documentary was out, and the world had seen it. But the fight for the truth was far from over.

After watching the documentary, I tried to rationalize their approach and even defended it publicly to an extent. I understood that the documentary was intended to honor Steve McNair's life and career, but with his and Jenny's tragic deaths being such a major—if not the biggest—part of the story, it was hard not to feel disappointed with how little time was dedicated to that portion.

Many people close to me shared their frustration, and the more they voiced their opinions, the more I started to see the gaps for myself. It almost felt like the controversy was intentionally avoided. They briefly touched on some of it in Vincent Hill's segment, but the majority of what I had shared was left out. It was puzzling why they chose to go that route.

Viewers expressed their frustrations as well. Many felt the documentary left them with more questions than answers. While die-hard football fans and Titans fans appreciated the football-focused segments, most people tuned in looking for clarity on the puzzling details surrounding the case. That clarity never came.

Shortly after the documentary's release, Joe and I started talking again. He was frustrated with how the documentary had been handled and encouraged me to do a follow-up. He offered to join me to help clear up some of what had been left out. I told Joe I didn't want to go online bashing anyone, especially since everyone involved in the production had been respectful to me throughout the process. However, I did feel the need to answer questions from those who had watched it.

As the messages and comments started to pile up—people asking for answers and expressing their disappointment—I knew I had to do something. I told Joe I was down for a follow-up, and we quickly put together another episode addressing the documentary. We gave our honest opinions and did our best to answer as many questions as possible.

Looking back now, I had truly hoped that the documentary would be the final time this situation needed to be addressed. I wanted it to tell the whole story, leaving no stone unturned and no detail left out. Unfortunately, that wasn't the case. For whatever reason, Netflix chose to go in a different direction. Instead of providing clarity, the documentary left many of the controversial questions unanswered, and now, those questions had only multiplied —with everyone looking to me to answer them.

As I reflected on the documentary and the criticism it received, several questionable details stood out to me—

both things I already knew and new insights I gained through the process, particularly from speaking to Vincent Hill and reading his book A Playbook to a Murder.

One of the biggest things that has never sat right with me—or anyone, for that matter—was just how quickly this case was closed. The police ruled it a murder-suicide in just four days, as if they were in a hurry to move on without thoroughly investigating. That alone raises so many red flags. High-profile cases like this usually involve extensive forensic reviews, ballistics tests, and deeper questioning of those involved. But in this case, it felt like the authorities locked in on a narrative immediately and refused to consider any alternatives.

Another major issue is Jenny's supposed role in this crime. The more I've looked into it, the more it just doesn't add up for me. Jenny had no real experience with guns, I'm positive of this, yet we're expected to believe she fired multiple precise shots—including two in McNair's chest and two in his head—before cleanly executing herself? That's not how murder-suicides usually happen. The level of accuracy suggests something closer to an execution-style killing rather than a crime of passion in my opinion.

Then there's Adrian Gilliam, the man who sold Jenny the gun. His story changed multiple times, and he already had a criminal record involving murder. He lied about knowing Jenny and lied about just about everything else. After that using the excuse, he didn't want to tell the truth because his fiance was present. He literally texted Jenny a multitude of times leading up to that night and apparently was the last person to ever text her. Why weren't the police more interested in his involvement? Why wasn't he treated as a serious suspect instead of just someone who happened to sell her a gun? His shifting statements alone should have warranted deeper scrutiny.

And what about the physical evidence—or lack of it? The angle of the gunshot wounds doesn't perfectly match what's expected for a self-inflicted shot. Where were Jenny's fingerprints on the gun? Why haven't the full crime scene photos been released, even to McNair's own mother? If this case is so clear-cut, what's the reason for withholding critical evidence? They rely heavily on the fact that there was gunpowder residue on her hand, but it was labeled as "minor traces." That makes no sense to me because, based on all the research I've done, when a gun is fired, gunpowder residue is everywhere—not just "minor traces." Not to mention, the hand they said she used to shoot the gun was opposite to the side where her fatal gunshot wound was found in her temple. That means she would have had to take the gun and cross her own face in an unnatural position to shoot herself on the opposite side of her head. That defies logic, and I haven't found any reports of anyone ever doing that in history.

Beyond just the crime itself, I also can't ignore all the suspicious events leading up to that night. A few nights before the deaths, someone showed up at my door in the middle of the night, banging on it aggressively. I had no idea who they were or what they wanted, but it sounded like a grown man trying to bust my door down. They only ran off when I threatened that I had a weapon. I had an eyewitness there with me that night when it happened. I texted everyone I knew, asking if it was them. The last person I texted was Jenny. She replied, saying it was her, but she refused to talk about it and never responded again. When I later brought this to the attention of the officers investigating the case, it was brushed off. They told me there was "no way to prove" that it was actually Jenny who replied, implying that she might have already been dead and that someone else could have been texting me from her phone.

Around the same time, I started getting a strong feeling that I was being followed. At first, I brushed it off as paranoia, but now, in hindsight, it feels like there was more going on—like someone was watching and waiting.

Even Jenny herself seemed different in the days leading up to the murders. The night before it happened, she was visibly distracted, like something was weighing on her heavily. Was she afraid of something? Was she being threatened? And if she was, why is there zero indication that investigators even considered this angle?

Then there's what happened afterward. The sketchy description of how they were discovered and the fact that the man that discovered them, Wayne Neely was on camera in the documentary himself offering the investigators hush money. Also why did it take so long for anyone to call the police and why did Neely call Gaddy instead of the police? Then there's the stalking outside my apartment by a black SUV on multiple nights following the investigation that later matched the description of Robert Gaddy's SUV, which was also seen near the crime scene. Also the neighbor's report of seeing two African American men running in and out of Jenny's apartment, carrying black trash bags full of items, and speeding off in a silver car—a car that was later determined to match the description of another car also belonging to Robert Gaddy. And then Jenny's apartment door was found wide open when everyone showed up to check on her, including myself and my family. All of this was ignored.

And then there's the conversation I had with Jenny shortly before everything happened, when we briefly started dating again. She told me she wanted to tell McNair's wife about their relationship. Even though I discouraged her, explaining why it was a bad idea, I still believe she went through with it. Later, in conversation with Vincent Hill and after reading his book, I learned that he had heard from a former friend of McNair's wife that she knew about Jenny—and that she wasn't happy about her. While this was never confirmed, it definitely strengthened my belief that Jenny likely told her.

When you piece all of this together—the execution-style shooting, the rushed investigation, the ignored alternative suspects, and the suppressed evidence—it feels like a cover-up rather than an honest attempt at finding the truth. The media and police crafted the public narrative in a way that was too convenient. Jenny was labeled as a jealous girlfriend who snapped, and that was that. Meanwhile, they sat on evidence that ruled me out for over a month before clearing my name, allowing speculation to spread like wildfire.

Even McNair's own mother doesn't believe Jenny did this, and yet, her questions—just like mine—have been met with silence. If this case is truly solved, why wouldn't the authorities want to be fully transparent, especially with the victim's own family?

So when I look at all of this—the rushed conclusion, the suspicious gun sale, the unexplored leads, the conflicting evidence, and the strange events leading up to and following the murders—I just can't accept the official story. The documentary confirmed some of the doubts I already had, but it also made me realize just how many details never made sense.

As time passed, I found myself reflecting more and more on the unanswered questions surrounding Jenny and what happened in 2009. The conversations that sparked after the documentary's release, the criticism it received, and the realization of just how many critical details were left unaddressed all weighed heavily on me. The more I thought about it, the more I realized that the story has never been told in its entirety.

I had started my own podcast, Life Through My Lens, where I talked about my personal experiences—everything I had been through, both the highs and the lows. Naturally, the topic of Jenny and 2009 came up again, and as I shared my thoughts, I started getting messages and comments from friends, family and listeners suggesting that I should consider writing a book. The idea intrigued me. In a way, it felt like a new creative outlet, something that could replace the way I had once used music to express myself. But at the same time, I hesitated.

I had always admired great books, but writing one myself felt overwhelming. I wasn't sure if I could find the right words to tell this story properly, in the way it needed to be told. The doubts crept in – Could I even do it justice? Where do I even begin?

But the more time passed, the more the idea stayed with me. It wouldn't let go. I started looking into my options, reaching out to authors and publishers, hoping for some insight. While many never responded, some did—and a few were even encouraging. They let me know that my story was compelling, that it deserved to be told, and that if I had the passion to share it, I should see it through.

At first, I considered the idea of having someone else write it for me, thinking I could simply provide the information and let a professional shape it into a book. But I quickly realized that wasn't the right path. It would be a long, expensive process, and more importantly, I knew deep down that no one else could tell my story the way I could.

So after weeks of conversations, reflection, and encouragement from those closest to me, I finally made my decision—I was going to write this book myself.

I had no idea how long it would take, or how well it would turn out. But I knew one thing for sure: the story needed to be told the right way, once and for all. And the only way my side of the story was ever going to be told properly was if I told it myself.

As I began the process of writing this book, I knew I needed a plan. I didn't want to be all over the place, jumping from thought to thought without structure. I had to outline everything carefully to ensure that I told the story in a way that made sense, not just for myself, but for anyone who would eventually read it.

I decided to start with my backstory, explaining what led me to leave my hometown and move to Florida in the first place. That was an important part of understanding who I was before I met Jenny, before everything changed. From there, I would introduce Jenny—not just the person the media portrayed, but who she really was. I wanted people to know why she meant so much to me, how we fell in love, and what made our relationship special.

I also knew I had to explain how our relationship came to an end, because that ultimately led to her ever meeting Steve McNair in the first place. This wasn't just about retelling old memories—it was about putting all the pieces together, laying everything out exactly as I knew it.

From there, I would cover everything I knew leading up to what happened, as well as everything I experienced in the aftermath. But as I wrote, I realized something else was just as important—I needed to talk about my life beyond that tragedy.

After a lot of thought, I knew I couldn't just stop the story there. I needed to share the struggles I faced in the years that followed—my marriage, my battles with emotional trauma, and the ways I tried to escape it. I had made mistakes, and I knew I wasn't alone in that. If this book could help even one person avoid leaning on the wrong things as a crutch—if it could redirect someone toward healing instead of suppression—then writing it would be worth it.

For years, I had bottled everything up, carrying it with me like an anchor that refused to let me move forward. Writing this book became an outlet I had spent years searching for, and even though revisiting some of these memories was beyond difficult, there was a sense of peace in finally getting it all out.

I still miss Jenny every day. There are a million things I wish I would have done differently, but there's nothing I can change now. A part of my heart was buried with her, and she will always be with me in my heart.

Because the truth is, when you truly love someone and you lose them, that love never goes away. It may fade over time, but you'll love them forever.

As far as closure goes, I'm honestly at a point in my life where I question whether it even exists. Not to sound negative—I hope that it does—but I've spent years hearing people talk about the things you can do to "find closure," and the truth is, I've never personally found it. At this point, I don't even know if I'm looking for it anymore.

Instead, I've accepted that what I went through was heartbreaking, life-altering, and something no one should ever have to experience. But the fact remains: I fell in love with Jenny, and I was still in love with her when she tragically passed away.

For years, I searched for ways to eliminate the pain, thinking that maybe if I could just move past it, I would finally feel "healed." But what I ultimately realized is that the only way to make the pain disappear would be if I had never truly loved or missed Jenny in the first place—and that simply wasn't true. I was trying to do something that couldn't be done.

It took me years to understand this, and for a long time, I carried a deep sense of guilt—especially when I remarried. I loved my wife, but at the same time, I still loved Jenny. I felt like that was wrong, like I was supposed to have moved on completely. But I shouldn't have felt guilty at all.

Because the truth is, I loved them both—but in completely different ways. And that's okay.

It took me so long to figure this out, but when I finally did, the answer was simple:

It's okay that I will always love Jenny.

It's okay that I still miss her.

And it's okay to fall in love again while feeling that way.

For most of my life, I put love in a box, believing that you could only love one person, one specific way. I held myself —and others—to that impossible standard. But it's simply not true.

So when I think about closure, I don't think I'll ever truly have it—and that's okay.

I've come to terms with the fact that the pain of losing Jenny will always be there.

And in a way, I wouldn't want it any other way.

Because she meant too much to me.

And she will always be worth it.

ABOUT THE AUTHOR

Keith Norfleet never set out to be a writer, but life had other plans. After many of his personal life experiences including love, heartbreak, and unimaginable loss, he turned to writing as a way to process his story. Beyond the Shadows is the result of a deeply personal account of the moments that changed everything.

Originally from Antioch, Tennessee, Keith is a devoted father, creative writer, and storyteller at heart. When he's not writing, he's focused on what matters most, his children and the life they continue to build together.

www.ingramcontent.com/pod-product-compliance
Lightning Source LLC
Chambersburg PA
CBHW070608030426
42337CB00020B/3712